T0196646

SHAMBHALA DRAGON EDITIONS

The dragon is an age-old symbol of the highest spiritual
essence, embodying wisdom, strength, and the divine power
of transformation. In this spirit, Shambhala Dragon Editions
offers a treasury of readings in the sacred knowledge of Asia.
In presenting the works of authors both ancient and modern,
we seek to make these teachings accessible to lovers of
wisdom everywhere.

The Dawn of Tantra

Herbert V. Guenther
and Chögyam Trungpa

edited by Michael Kohn

illustrated by Glen Eddy
and Terris Temple

Shambhala
Boston & London
2001

SHAMBHALA PUBLICATIONS, INC.
Horticultural Hall
300 Massachusetts Avenue
Boston, Massachusetts 02115
www.shambhala.com

Printed in the United States of America
⊗This edition is printed on acid-free paper that meets
the American National Standards Institute z39.48 Standard.
Distributed in the United States by Random House, Inc.,
and in Canada by Random House of Canada Ltd

The Library of Congress catalogues the previous
edition of this book as follows:

Guenther, Herbert V.
The dawn of tantra
1. Tantric Buddhism—Addresses, essays, lecturers.
I. Chögyam Trungpa, Trungpa Tulku, 1939–. II. Title.
BQ8916.G83   294.5'92   74-10250
ISBN 0-87773-059-8 (pbk.)
ISBN 1-57062-896-3 (pbk.)

Contents

ONE   *Tantra: Its Origin and Presentation*   1

TWO   *Laying the Foundation*   6

THREE   *Yogacara and the Primacy of Experience*   12

FOUR   *The Mandala Principle and the Meditative Process*   21

FIVE   *The Indivisibility of Openness and Compassion*   26

SIX   *The Development of Shunyata*   34

SEVEN   *The Guru-Disciple Relationship*   41

EIGHT   *Visualization*   47

NINE   *Empowerment and Initiations*   53

TEN   *Questions and Answers: Guenther*   63

ELEVEN   *Questions and Answers: Rinpoche*   78

Chapters One, Three, Five, Seven, Nine and Ten are by Herbert V. Guenther

Chapters Two, Four, Six, Eight and Eleven are by Chogyam Trungpa

Illustrations

page x   PADMA SAMBHAVA (central figure), dGa'-Rab-rDo-rJe (upper figure). *Glen Eddy*

page 20   MARPA (central figure), Two-armed Hevajra (upper figure). *Terris Temple*

page 40   NAROPA. *Glen Eddy.*

page 46   MAHAVAIROCANA (central figure), Vajradhara (upper figure). *Terris Temple*

page 93   mGON-PO-LEGS-lDAN (the 'Grandfather' Mahakala). *Glen Eddy*

Introduction

WESTERNERS wanting to know about tantra, particularly the Buddhist tantra of Tibet, have had to work with speculation and fancy. Tibet has been shrouded in mystery; "tantra" has been called upon to name every kind of esoteric fantasy; Buddhism has been left either vague or inaccessible. Academic treatments have been of little help, being in the main inaccurate or remote, failing either to comprehend or to convey.

In *The Dawn of Tantra* the reader meets a Tibetan and a Westerner whose grasp of Buddhist tantra is real and unquestionable. Dr. Guenther holds Ph.D. degrees from the Universities of Munich and Vienna. In 1950, he went to India to teach at Lucknow University and, in 1958, became Head of the Department of Comparative Philosophy and Buddhist Studies at the Sanskrit University in Varanasi. Since 1964, he has been Head of the Department of Far Eastern Studies at the University of Saskatchewan in Canada. Because of his tremendous intellectual energy and scholarly discipline, knowledge of Tibetan, Sanskrit and Chinese, and his years of collaboration with native Tibetans, he has become one of the few Westerners to penetrate to a deeper understanding of Tibetan tantric texts. His books, such as *The Life and Teaching of Naropa* and the *Tantric View of Life,* bring us nearly the only accurate translations and commentaries from the Tibetan Buddhist tradition.

Chögyam Trungpa was born in the heart of the Buddhist

tantra tradition. As the eleventh incarnation of the Trungpa line of spiritual teachers, he was enthroned at the age of eighteen months as abbot of a group of monasteries in eastern Tibet. Beginning at three, he underwent intensive training in the intellectual and meditative disciplines of Buddhism. He had completely assumed his responsibilities, both spiritual and temporal, by the age of fourteen and went on to become a master of tantric Buddhist meditation. His journey towards the West began in 1959 when he fled the Chinese Communist invasion of Tibet. He first experienced the modern world in India, where he spent four years studying English. Since then he has traversed the West. He studied comparative religion at Oxford and founded a meditation center in Scotland. He arrived in the United States in 1970, where he has published several books, among them *Cutting Through Spiritual Materialism,* founded a number of meditation centers, a community working in art and theatre, and another for helping the mentally disturbed, based on tantric principles. He has not remained cloistered, but has fully and frankly encountered the Western mind on the learned and gut levels. He has mastered English to the level of poetry.

Having worked towards each other, so to speak, for years, Dr. Guenther and Chögyam Trungpa met in Berkeley, California, in 1972, where together they gave a public seminar on Buddhist tantra. *Dawn of Tantra* is the edited record of that seminar including part of the general discussion. The "Visualization" chapter is from a seminar given by Trungpa in San Francisco in 1973. The "Empowerment and Initiation" chapter is from a talk given by Dr. Guenther when he visited Trungpa's meditation center in Boulder, Colorado, in 1973. Dr. Guenther has also since lectured at Naropa Institute, a university founded by Trungpa in Boulder, Colorado.

Guenther and Trungpa are an interface very much alive to the Tibetan tradition of Buddhist tantra and very much alive to the current everyday world of America. They communicate warmly and freely in both directions and give no quarter to wishful thinking.

Michael H. Kohn

The Dawn of Tantra

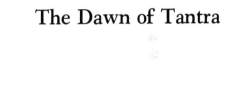

CHAPTER ONE

Tantra: Its Origin and Presentation

THE term *tantra,* from the time of its first appearance in the West up to the present day, has been subject to serious misunderstandings. The term was introduced into the English language in 1799 when tantric works were discovered by missionaries in India. These were not Buddhist works. In fact at that time it was hardly known in the West that such a thing as Buddhism existed. The term tantra was then known only as the title of these works, the contents of which was quite different from what people expected in books dealing with philosophy and religion. The missionaries were for the most part quite shocked that other people had religious and philosophical ideas so different from their own. To them the word tantra meant no more than these expanded treatises; but since the subject matter dealt with in these treatises was so unusual from their point of view, the term began to acquire quite a peculiar connotation, a connotation which proper study of the texts has not borne out. Unfortunately, in this case as in so many others, once a false conception has been formed, a nearly superhuman effort is required to root out and set right all the wrong ideas and odd connotations that have grown up

1

around it. I am going to try to tell you what the term tantra actually means in a technical sense.

First of all, one must distinguish between the tantra of the Hinduist tradition and the tantra of the Buddhist tradition. These two traditions, both indigenous to India, for a long period of time used the same language—Sanskrit. But each tradition stipulated particular uses for its terms. What one tradition understood by a specific term was not necessarily what the other tradition understood by it. When Buddhist studies originated in the West, which was only comparatively recently, it was assumed by the first investigators that since the Buddhists used the same Sanskrit terms as the Hindus, they would mean the same thing by them. This was the first of many wrong conclusions that they drew.

Let us apply ourselves to an understanding of tantra as it developed in the Buddhist tradition. A term that has been used from the beginning in close association with the term tantra is the Sanskrit *prabandha*. Prabandha means continuity. This is a continuity of being, which divides into two grounds: we have to start somewhere, and then go a certain way (and perhaps arrive at a goal). This is the way tantra was presented. It refers to an immediate human situation which arises out of the question of how we are going to *be*. Tantra also sees the question of how we are going to be in terms of relationship, realizing that man is always related to something or someone.

Tantra approaches the question of being in various ways; thus there is more than one presentation of it. The first approach is called *Kriyatantra*. In the Kriyatantra the emphasis is on how a person acts. *Kriya* means "action." Action is here seen symbolically and dealt with in terms of ritual. We need not be mystified by the idea of ritual. An example of ritual is the custom of a man's removing his hat when he meets a lady. It is a kind of formalized gesture. It is also a way of going about a human relationship. The emphasis in the Kriyatantra is on relationship as expressed in this kind of formalized gesture. In this case the emphasis is far-reaching and covers many aspects of relationship. The Kriyatantra is further particularized in its approach to human relationship in that it deals with the simplest and earliest stages of it.

The earliest form of relationship is that of a child with his parents. There is a kind of dominance involved here. Someone has to tell the child what and what not to do. When this relational situation is transferred into a religious context it becomes the idea that man is subject to a transcendental entity. This is perhaps the generally accepted idea and it is also the framework in the Kriyatantra. Here the practitioner tries to gain favor with the one with whom he is interrelated. This and the strong ritualistic emphasis are two main charac teristics of the Kriyatantra. This tantra also stresses purification. The ritual includes various ablutions. Some of them are purely symbolic in importance and perhaps the sense of cleanliness involved might seem somewhat exaggerated. We must realize, however, that the sense of being clean can become extremely important in an emotional context such as this one. It has a much more profound significance than in ordinary circumstances when someone says: "Now before you eat, wash your hands." So this emphasis on purity is another characteristic of Kriyatantra.

But man is not content with merely being told what to do. He is also a thinking being and will ask questions. And here is where a further approach to tantra, known as the *Caryatantra* comes in. Again here, tantra refers to a relational situation. But here the emphasis has shifted. We are no longer only concerned with following certain accepted rules of relationship, but also to a certain extent with understanding the implications of them. This marks the entry of a certain questioning of ourselves. Why are we doing these things? Why do we behave in such-and-such a way? Certainly we do not discard our behavior at this point, but we ask about its significance. And this we do by thinking more about it. We try to gain insight into it and this can be a kind of meditation.

Here there begins to be a balance between thought and action. This change from the previous mere acceptance of authority corresponds to a change in the character of our relationship with the one to whom we are relating. It is no longer a question of a master telling his servant or slave what to do. There is now more of a feeling of intimacy, of comradeship, more of an equal status. The one is still willing to learn, but the other now realizes that he is in the same situation as the first. It is a relationship of friendship and friendship can only be based on an acceptance of the other person in his or her own right. Servitude makes friendship impossible.

But friendship can be developed still further than this first intimacy. Friendship often entails our trying to find out more about the relationship. What is valuable about this relationship that compels us to cultivate it? This questioning process leads to the further development of insight. The emphasis has shifted again. This new aspect of the total situation of how we are together brings us into the *Yogatantra*.

The term *yoga* has many meanings. In the Buddhist context, it means "to harness." It is etymologically related to the English word yoke. It means to harness everything in us in order to gain more insight. Thus the situation, the tantra, in which this is the emphasis is called the Yogatantra. Here there is a teamwork which is even better than that between two friends. But there is still room for further development because we still consider the other slightly different from ourselves. This is where the fourth division, the *Mahayogatantra,* comes in.

Maha basically means "great," but here it is used not so much to mean great as opposed to small, but with the sense that there could be nothing greater. It is used in an absolute sense. The Mahayogatantra partakes of this sense of absoluteness in its approach to the situation of relationship. We no longer make any distinctions; we just are, spontaneous, free. The question of whether or not the other is my friend no longer arises. There is a complete unity—we are just one.

So there is a progression in the tantras, beginning from the level of a child related to its parents and developing to the level of complete maturity. Thus when we use the term tantra, we not only refer to a particular situation, but we also describe a process of growth, a process of inner development which takes place when we try to understand what there is. This process goes on until we come to the proper assessment of experience, the proper way of seeing. There is a dialectical relationship between action, the way in which we behave, and the insight we have attained. The more we know, the more we learn about another person, the more responsive we become to that person. We begin to realize what he needs and stop imposing the idea of what we think he should need. We begin to be able to help that person find his own way.

This leads us to the practical significance of tantra. Tantra, as a way of inner growth, makes us see more, so that we really become individuals rather than mere entities in an amorphous context. But tantra goes still further. It goes beyond the idea of a growth or a progress. There are further stages and subdivisions within the tradition, which deal with the fact that even after we have learned to relate properly to our problems, life still goes on. The idea here is that spiritual practice is a continual movement. It is only from the point of view of discursive thought that we begin somewhere, progress or develop, and then reach a certain goal. It is not as though, having found enlightenment, the process is completed and everything comes to an end. Rather, the fact is that we continue to live, so we must continually start anew. Nevertheless, through the previous stages, we have found a way, a way of relating, a certain continuity. This continuity of a way of relating is the basic meaning of tantra. In a sense this is an extremely simple point. In general, however, we find that there is scarcely anything more difficult than this kind of simplicity.

CHAPTER TWO

Laying the Foundation

Professor Guenther and I decided that the best way for us to approach the subject of tantra together is for him to deal with the *prajna* or knowledge aspect of it and for me to deal with the *upaya,* the skillful means or actual application aspect of it.

From the practical side then, the basic idea of tantra is, like any other teaching of Buddhism, the attainment of enlightenment. But in tantra the approach to enlightenment is somewhat different. Rather than aiming at the attainment of the enlightened state, the tantric approach is to see the continuity of enlightened mind in all situations, as well as the constant discontinuity of it.

Experience on the tantric level corresponds to the utmost and most complete state of being that can be attained. On the other hand, tantra is not a question of attainment, but rather the actual work of relating to situations properly.

All kinds of emphasis has been laid on the various colorful attributes of tantra. One speaks of its ten special aspects. There is the *sadhana,* that is, the method or practice; there are the practices of meditation; there is the realization of one's innate nature through identifying with various deities; and so on. The basic nature of tantra can be defined in terms of ten such ways in which it differs from sutra teachings.

6

The tantric teaching is divided into the three categories of *dharmakaya, sambhogakaya* and *nirmanakaya.* All tantric teachings have these three aspects. The teaching of tantra in terms of the three kayas can also be related to the three main vehicles of Buddhism. The nirmanakaya aspect of tantra is associated with the Hinayana, the way of monastic discipline. The sambhogakaya aspect of tantra could be said to be its Mahayana aspect; it is concerned with various yogic practices dealing with *prana, bindu, nadis* and so on. The dharmakaya or Vajrayana aspect of tantra is concerned with pure being or suchness. In Tibetan this is referred to as *de-kho-na-nyid,* "that which is, that which just simply is." This is the ultimate aspect of the tantric teaching. Nevertheless, the basic quality of continuity continues even beyond this.

The Tibetan names for sutra and tantra give some insight into the difference between the two kinds of teaching. The Tibetan for sutra is *mdo,* which means "confluence" or "junction." It is a point where things can meet, coincide, conclude together. Most simply, it is the place where the teachings can come together with the problems of everyday life. Take the conclusions of the Four Noble Truths: suffering, the origin of suffering, the cessation of suffering and the path. These are conclusions that coincide with all kinds of human conflicts of mind. Tantra, as we know, means "continuity," which is something more than just junction. From the tantric viewpoint, the junction of the sutras is not important. Junction is just the sparkling experience of insight, a sudden glimpse of something that comes together because two aspects of all experience suddenly are in a chaotic relationship from the point of view of the ordinary ego-oriented set-up. Hate and love, to take the example of emotions, come together. The solidity of hate, which depends on ego's set-up, encounters the ego quality of love. Suddenly, both hate and love are there together and suddenly love does not exist and hate does not exist. The ego ground of the situation is exploded. So aspects of the situation come together and there is a flow. At the moment of coming together, there is an explosion, which is actually the discovery of truth.

Tantra does not lay strong emphasis on this moment of the discovery of truth, because it is not so interested in truth as opposed to confusion. Rather the principle of tantra is the continuity which runs through both truth and confusion. In Tibetan tantra is called *rgyud,* which is like the thread which runs through beads. It continues from the beginning through the middle and the end. One speaks of the basic ground of tantra as continuity, the continuity as the path of tantra, and the continuity as the fruition of tantra. So tantra starts at the beginning, continues on the path and ends at the goal or fruition. But it does not exactly end at that point. In terms of the practice it ends; in terms of attainment it does not end. There is still the play of what is called Buddha-activity. The general picture is that you attain the experiences first of nirmanakaya, then sambhogakaya, then dharmakaya. Then having mastered the ultimate experiences, Buddha-activity begins and you work back down from dharmakaya to sambhogakaya to nirmanakaya. Having achieved the peak experiences, you come back down in order to relate with sentient beings, people who are confused, relate with them through speech or through body or whatever may be appropriate. You speak the same language as they do. So tantra goes beyond the fruition level.

In the tantric tradition, ego or confusion or ignorance is personified as *Rudra.* All the tantric traditions of Buddhism are concerned with the taming of Rudra, the Rudra of ego. The Rudra principle is divided, especially in the Atiyoga tradition, into the ego of the body, the ego of the speech and the ego of the mind. This means the fixation or appropriation of the elements of body, speech and mind by the ego in relation to its security or expansion. In speaking of the fixation of the body, we are not referring to purely physical attachment—lust, let's say—as a purely physical matter. We are talking about the mind-body situation, the body aspect of our mind, the solidity aspect of it which needs constant feeding, reinforcement. It needs continual reassurance that it is solid. That is the Rudra of the body.

The Rudra of speech is the fixation of the element which is related with both the body and the mind but at the same time is uncertain which. This is a fickleness or wavering quality, uncertain whether one's foundation is the fixed aspect of the body—the physical level of the textures and colors of life—or perhaps the emotional situation of whether to love or to hate.

This uncertain wavering back and forth, this fickleness quality, is speech (or mantra, if you prefer), the voice. The fixation of this is the Rudra of speech.

The Rudra of mind is fundamentally believing that, if a higher state of spiritual development is to be attained, it has to be manufactured rather than uncovered. Rangjung Dorje, a great teacher of the Kagyü tradition, in his commentary on the *Hevajra Tantra,* says that the ultimate materialism is believing that Buddha-nature can be manufactured by mental effort, spiritual gymnastics. So that is psychological and spiritual materialism—the Rudra of the mind.

These three principles—the fixation and solidification of the security of the body; the fixation on the emotional level of being uncertain but still hanging onto something; the fixation on the mental level of believing in some ultimate savior principle, some principle outside one's own nature that, so to speak, can do the trick—these three principles of Rudra constitute one of the prime occupations of tantra, which is concerned with overcoming them.

The three Rudra principles also correspond to the threefold division of tantra. At the beginning, in order to relate to the Rudra of body, the student must begin tantric study on the Hinayana level. This includes practices such as the *satipatthana* practices, which the Hinayana developed for training the mind. These practices concentrate on breathing, walking and other bodily movements. They simplify the basic nature of solidity. This can be understood if we realize that this kind of solidifying by the ego of its space is based on an attitude which trusts complexity. It places its trust on very complicated answers, complicated logic. Satipatthana is a way of simplifying the logical mind, which is body in this case, because it relates to something very solid and definite. The logical mind attempts to fixate, hold onto, grasp and thus is continually projecting something definite and solid. So the basic Hinayana practice of simplifying every activity of the mind into just breathing or bodily movement reduces the intensity of the Rudra of body. It does not particularly transcend it or free one from it, but at least it reduces the intensity of it.

The next stage, dealing with the Rudra of speech, is on the sambhogakaya level. All kinds of practices have developed for this in the Tibetan tradition. Notably, there is what is known as the four foundation practices: one hundred thousand prostrations, one hundred thousand repetitions of the refuge formula, one hundred thousand repetitions of the hundred-syllable Vajrasattva mantra, and one hundred thousand offerings of one's body, speech and mind as the whole universe. These preliminary tantric practices on the sambhogakaya level are related with prana, nadis, and bindu. They are based on making use of the speed, the movement, the rhythm of confused mind. At the same time, there is something very unconfused about these practices. One cannot go through them all without relating to the true nature of body, speech and mind. They occupy a sort of intermediary place between confusion and clarity. And the basic continuity principle of tantra underlies the whole thing.

Having gone through the satipatthana of the Hinayana or nirmanakaya level (which includes the *samatha* and *vipassana* practices), having completed the four foundation practices on the Mahayana or sambhogakaya level, the student is now just ready to have a glimpse of the guru, of real relationship and practice with the guru, real commitment to the guru. This is where the guru yoga practice for attaining union with the guru comes in. When that has been completed, then comes what is called *abhisheka,* which could be translated as "initiation" or "confirmation." This is the entry to the dharmakaya level.

There are four levels of abhisheka and all take place within a realm of space in which the student and teacher meet in some basic understanding. This understanding is the result of the previous practices. The student has related to his body, learned to slow down the speed of muscles, veins, emotions, blood. Circulations of all kinds have been slowed down altogether. Now the student is finally able to relate to the ultimate space through his relationship and union with the teacher. In the Zen tradition this is known as transmission. It seems to be the same meeting of two minds as is found in tantra.

We can see from this brief look that the practice of tantra is not easy. The student has to begin at the beginning. He has to acquire an understanding of the principle of taming the mind. Understanding of the Rudra principle brings egolessness or Rudralessness. He has to get to know his own bodily situation through the preliminary tantric practices. Then he can achieve the final surrendering through abhisheka. Looked at as a whole, the practice of tantra is like building a house. First you put down the foundation, then you build the first story, then the second. Then you can put a gold roof on it if you like. We have looked at the sutra or Hinayana aspect within tantra, the Mahayana aspect within tantra, then the final subtleties of tantra within itself. Looked at in this way, the whole of the practice of Buddhism can be regarded as tantra, although all Buddhists outside the historical tradition of tantra might not agree with this.

CHAPTER THREE

Yogacara and the Primacy of Experience

THE idea of tantra as continuity connects this inquiry with the philosophy of the Yogacara since this early Indian school of Buddhist philosophy was instrumental in developing the idea of tantra.

The Yogacara school was so named because its philosophy leads to application, working on oneself—yoga, harnessing. It has been called by various names in the West, one of the most common (also known in Japan) being *cittamatra,* which is usually translated "mind-only." Now the word "mind" is very nebulous in meaning, different people understanding different things by it. Let us try to understand how the Yogacara school understood this term.

The Yogacara system is not, strictly speaking, a single system, but embraces a number of philosophical trends which are in certain ways quite distinct from one another. They are lumped together under this title in virtue of the main tenet which they hold in common; the idea that all the three worlds (the world of sensuousness, the world of form, the world of formlessness) are cittamatra, mind only.

The word *citta* (mind), from early times was used to mean, not so much a container of thoughts, as perhaps we tend to understand it, but rather something like a clearinghouse that could both store and transmit impressions. It was thought of as something like a battery. It could be charged and then when it was charged it would do something. It had this double function which must be borne in mind if we wish to understand the idea of cittamatra. In the first place, since the concept of citta revolves around the storing and transmission of experience, it would be more precise to translate the idea of cittamatra as "experience alone counts."

Buddhism has always placed great emphasis on experience. The four basic axioms of Buddhism are highly experiential in character. The first is that everything is transitory; the second that everything is frustrating; the third that everything is without essence; the fourth that nirvana is bliss. These first three axioms relate very much to our actual way of going through life. We observe life and see that nothing lasts; we feel that being faced with trying to build something on this basis is very frustrating. Then we think and we ask ourselves, "How is this? Why is this?" We get the answer that if everything is transitory it cannot have an essence; because an essence is by definition the principle by which something is what it is. If we started reasoning from the idea of an essence, we could not account for transitoriness, nor could we account for the constant frustration which we experience.

Now the continual frustration makes us feel that some other mode of being must be possible. This is where we come to the fourth basic axiom, which says that nirvana is bliss. Buddha's disciple Ananda asked him how he could make such a statement, having said that feelings and all such forms are transitory. The Buddha replied that he had qualified nirvana as bliss only by way of language, that he did not thereby mean a judgment of feeling, such as when we call something pleasant. The term he used for bliss was *sukha*, which is very close to what we have referred to as the peak experience. This seems to be an experience in which all conceptions and judgments, even the idea of oneself, completely pass away. So what is referred to as bliss can be understood to transcend transitoriness or permanence or any other form. In later Buddhist philosophical systems, especially the tantra, we find that further developments concerning this state have taken place to the point where even the last trace of experience as such has disappeared. Even the possibility of saying, "I had thus-and-such an experience" has evaporated. This view was developed directly from the idea of the Yogacaras that "experience alone counts."

But the question still remains of how it comes about that we are always in the realm of frustration. Also, how can we understand the fact that our sense of continual frustration leads us to feel that there is some other mode of experience which gets rid of this frustration? To see the answers to these questions, we must go still further in our understanding of the term citta.

The Yogacaras developed an understanding of citta involving eight aspects. What they were actually trying to do was to describe the process in which citta emerges from its primordial, unqualified and unconditioned state and glides into our ordinary way of thinking. If we understood this process thoroughly, we would be able to do away with it and let our minds remain in the primordial state. This would be the peak experience.

In describing this process, the Yogacaras used the concept of the *alayavijnana,* a concept which has been used differently by different Buddhist schools and which is very important in the tantric tradition. The alayavijnana is already different from the *alaya* or basic foundation. The latter we assume for the purposes of communication, without affirming that it is an ontological entity. The alayavijnana is already a trend developing into the split we usually describe as subject and object. We see here that the citta is a dynamic factor rather than a static conception. In the function of the alayavijnana it is in constant transformation, developing into further dualistic forms.

Here we can see the influence of the old conception of citta as something which stores something up and, once this storage has reached its high point, must be discharged. This idea of stored potentialities of experience that must at some point be actualized is constantly present in Buddhist philosophy. The precise forms which cause the alayavijnana to function in this way are called *vasanas.* These are deposits that are potentialities. They develop according to two principles, the one a principle of intrinsic similarity, the other a principle of taking on various specific forms in accordance with conditions. For instance, a scientist, by way of experiment, might take some kidney cells and plant them on some other part of the body, say an arm. They will not develop as skin cells, but will continue to develop as kidney cells. This is the first principle. But the way in which these kidney cells develop as kidney cells will vary according to a multiplicity of conditions. Some people have kidney trouble and others do not. This illustrates the second principle.

As we have said, what develops in the course of the transformation of citta is a split. As the initial step in the genesis of experience from the process known as the alayavijnana, there develops something else, which is known as *manas* in Sanskrit and *yid* in Tibetan. This aspect of citta now looks back and takes the original unity out of which it developed as its real self. This original unity is what is taken as an ontologically real self by the Hindus.

The Hindus described the original unity as the transcendental ego and the manas as the empirical ego. The Buddhists rejected the reification of these aspects, having seen that they all belonged to the unity of a transformational process. According to the Yogacara, the split that occurs merely contrasts a limited form with a vital primordial form. The manas or yid then becomes the source of all subsequent mental functions in the way indicated by common speech when we say "I see" or "I think." But all these mental functions are part of the total process of transformation.

According to the Yogacara view, the original source (the alayavijnana) is undifferentiated and ethically or karmically neutral. When the split occurs it becomes tainted, but still the particular mental movement in question is not determined as ethically positive or negative. This determination takes place through elaborations of the movement which further specify it. This elaboration takes the form of our perceiving with the five senses, and also with the traditional Buddhist sixth sense, which we might loosely call consciousness; that is, the categorical perception which brings categories into sense data without abstracting them from it. Thus the alayavijnana, the manas and the six senses are the eight aspects of citta.

This process of transformation we have described is one of growing narrowness and frozenness. We are somehow tied down to our senses, to the ordinary mode of perception. We dimly feel that something else might have been possible. If we try to express this situation in traditional religious terms, we might say that man is a fallen being. But here he has not fallen because he has sinned or transgressed some commandment coming from outside him, but by the very fact that he has moved in a certain direction. This is technically known in Buddhism as *bhranti* in Sanskrit or *'khrul-pa* in Tibetan, and is usually translated as "error." But error implies, in Western thinking, culpability; and there is absolutely no culpability involved. We might tend to feel that we could have done otherwise, but this attitude simply does not apply here. The process is a kind of going astray which just happens. The idea of sin is irrelevant.

Still we have the feeling of something gone wrong. If we accept our ordinary experience as error, then we ask the question "Is true knowledge possible?" Now the very question already implies that it is possible. That is to say, the sense of error implies the sense of truth. We could not know error without unerring knowledge. So there is this oscillation back and forth between error and knowledge; and this oscillation presents the possibility of returning to what we have referred to as the original or primordial state.

Here original does not have the sense of "beginning." We speak of it as the original state because we feel that our charge of creative power came from there. We experienced an energy which we felt to be of the highest value, quite distinct from the tone of our ordinary experience. The existential apprehension of this original state is technically known in the tantric tradition as the *mahasukhakaya*.

In the ordinary Buddhist tradition there is the nirmanakaya, sambhogakaya and dharmakaya. Then if it is wished to emphasize the unity of the three and avoid any tendency to concretize them as separate, we speak of the whole as the svabhavikakaya. This is not a fourth kaya, but the unity of the three. The mahasukhakaya is a significant addition to this picture which came in with tantra. *Sukha* means "bliss"; *maha* means "than which there could be none greater." So we have the peak experience again; and this is always felt as being, which gives kaya.

Kaya is translated as "body," but not in the sense of the purely physical abstraction which is often made in defining "body," where we say that one thing is the mental aspect of us and the other thing is the physical aspect. This is a misconception. There is no such thing as a body without a mind. If we have a body without a mind, it is not a body, it is a corpse. It is a mere object to be disposed of. If we speak properly of a body, we mean something which is alive; and we cannot have a live body without a mind. So the two cannot be separated—they go together.

Thus the mahasukhakaya is an existential factor, which is of the highest value. This is not an arbitrary assignment of value that is made here. It is just felt that this is the only absolute value. This absolute value can be retrieved by reversing the process of error, of going astray; by reverting the energy that flows in one direction and becomes frozen, less active. It is this process of freezing which causes us to feel imprisoned and tied down. We are no longer free agents, as it were, but are in samsara.

So in answer to the question of whether or not there is some alternative to the continual frustration in which we live, the answer is, yes. Let us find the initial, original, primordial, or whatever word you want to use—language is so limited—as a value. This is the mahasukhakaya.

The possibility of returning to the origin has been rendered manifest in the form of certain symbols of transformation, such as the mandala. Transformation from ordinary perception to primordial intrinsic awareness can take place when we try to see things differently, perhaps somewhat as an artist does. Every artist knows that he can see in two different ways. The ordinary way is characterized by the fact that perception is always related to accomplishing some end other than the perception itself. It is treated as a means rather than something in itself. But we can also look at things and enjoy their presence aesthetically.

If we look at a beautiful sunset, we can look at it as a physicist does and see it as a system of wavelengths. We lose the feeling of it completely. We can also look at it as a poignant symbol of the impermanence of all things and be moved to sadness. But this also is not just the sunset itself. There is a definite difference when we just look at it as it is and enjoy the vast play of colors that is there in tremendous vividness. When we look like this, we will immediately notice how free we become. The entire network of mental factors in which we usually labor just drops off. Everyone can do this but, of course, it requires work.

The art of the mandala has been developed to help us see things in their intrinsic vividness. Although all mandalas are fundamentally similar, each is also unique. The colors used in them, for instance, vary greatly according to the basic make-up of the practitioners. The character of a particular mandala is known as the *dhatu-tathagatagarbha*. *Dhatu* here refers to the factor of the particular individual make-up. *Tathagatagarbha* refers to the awakened state of mind or Buddhahood. So a particular mandala could be seen as a specific index of the awakened state of mind. Care is taken to relate to individual characteristics because, although each person is capable of total Buddhahood, he must start from the aspect of it that is most strongly present in him.

There is a Zen saying that even a blade of grass can become a Buddha. How are we to understand this? Usually we consider that a blade of grass simply belongs to the physical world; it is not even a sentient being, since it has no feelings, makes no judgments, has no perceptions. The explanation is that everything is of the nature of Buddha, so grass is also of this nature. It is not that it in some way contains Buddha-nature, that we can nibble away analytically at the various attributes of the blade of grass until there is nothing left but some vague leftover factor that we then pigeonhole as Buddha-nature. Rather, the blade of grass actually constitutes what we call Buddhahood or an ultimate value.

It is in this sense that a blade of grass or any other object can be a symbol of transformation. The whole idea of symbols of transformation is made possible by the philosophical development of the Yogacaras, who saw that what comes to us in earthly vessels, as it were, the elements of our ordinary experience, *is* the fundamental mind, the ultimate value. The ultimate value comes in forms intelligible to us. Thus certain symbols such as mandalas, already partially intelligible to us, can be used as gateways to the peak experience.

So these symbols exist, differing according to the needs of individuals. We can slip into the world of running around in circles—that is what *samsara* literally means—or we can also, through such symbols, find our way out of it. But the way out is nowhere else but in the world where we are. There is no other world besides the world we live in. This is one of the main purports of Buddhist philosophy and one which Westerners often find hard to grasp. Buddhist philosophy does not make the distinction between the phenomenal and the noumenal. The phenomenon is the noumenon and the noumenon is the phenomenon; not in the sense of mathematical equation, but in the sense that you cannot have one without the other. The technical statement of this is that there is appearance and there is also *shunyata;* but shunyata is not somewhere else, it is in the appearance. It is its open dimension. The appearance never really implies any restriction or limitation. If there were such a limitation, we could never get out of it.

CHAPTER FOUR

The Mandala Principle
and the Meditative Process

Tantra cannot be understood apart from experience arising out of the practice of meditation. Tantra, as we have said, can be regarded as the golden roof of the house. Before we can put on a roof, we have first to have built a house, and before that even, to have laid a foundation. I have already mentioned the four foundation practices. But such practices by themselves are not enough; we have to do the basic work of relating to ourselves. The work we must do to have a complete understanding of the symbolism of tantra and of the mandala principle begins at a very rudimentary level.

A mandala consists of a center and the fringe area of a circle. On the basic level, it consists of the practitioner and his relationship to the phenomenal world. The study of the mandala principle is that of the student in his life situation.

In a sense spiritual practice in Buddhism in the beginning stages could be said to be very intellectual. It is intellectual in the sense of being precise. It could also be seen as intellectual because of the nature of the dialogue which has to take place between the student and the teacher, the student and the teaching. A certain questioning process has to take place. It is not a matter of memorizing texts or merely applying a variety of techniques. Rather it is necessary that situations be created in which the student can relate to himself as a potential Buddha, as a dharma-body—he relates his whole psyche or whole make-up to the Dharma. He must begin with a precise study of himself and his situation.

Traditionally there are twelve types of teaching styles proper to a Buddha. The sutras can be divided into twelve categories according to which of the twelve styles the Buddha has employed in it. One of the twelve styles is that of creating a situation in which the teaching can transpire. Take the example of the *Prajnaparamitahridaya* or *Heart Sutra.* In the original Sanskrit version of this sutra, Buddha does not say a word; but it was Buddha who created the dialogue between Avalokiteshvara and Shariputra. Buddha created the situation in which Shariputra could act as the receiver or audience and Avalokiteshvara as the propounder of the analysis.

So creating the situation in which the student can relate to the teaching is the initial creation of the mandala principle. There is the hungry questioning, the thirsty mind which examines all possibilities. The questions are inspired by the basic suffering of the student's situation, the basic chaos of it. It is uncertainty, dissatisfaction, which brings out the questions.

Seen in the tantric perspective, the first stages of the creation of the mandala principle are the basic Buddhist practices on the Hinayana level. The starting point is samatha practice, which is the development of peace or dwelling on peace. This practice does not, however, involve dwelling or fixing one's attention on a particular thing. Fixation or concentration tends to develop trance-like states. But from the Buddhist point of view, the point of meditation is not to develop trance-like states; rather it is to sharpen perceptions, to see things as they are. Meditation at this level is relating with the conflicts of our life situations, like using a stone to sharpen a knife, the situation being the stone. The samatha meditation, the beginning point of the practice, could be described as sharpening one's knife. It is a way of relating to bodily sensations and thought processes of all kinds; just relating with them rather than dwelling on them or fixing on them in any way.

Dwelling or fixing comes from an attitude of trying to prove something, trying to maintain the "me" and "my" of ego's territory. One needs to prove that ego's thesis is secure. This is an attempt to ignore the samsaric circle, the samsaric whirlpool. This vicious circle is too painful a truth to accept, so one is seeking something else to replace it with. One seeks to replace the basic irritation or pain with the pleasure of a fixed belief in oneself by dwelling on something, a certain spiritual effort or just worldly things. It seems that, as something to be dwelled on, conceptualized ideas of religion or spiritual teachings or the domestic situations of life are extensions of the ego. One does not simply see tables and chairs as they are; one sees my manifestation of table, my manifestation of chair. One sees constantly the "me" or "my" in these things; they are seen constantly in relationship to me and my security.

It is in relation to this world of my projections that the precision of samatha is extremely powerful. It is a kind of scientific research, relating to the experiences of life as substances and putting them under the microscope of meditative practice. One does not dwell on them, one examines them, works with them. Here the curiosity of one's mind acts as potential prajna, potential transcendental knowledge. The attitude of this practice is not one of seeking to attain nirvana, but rather of seeing the mechanism of samsara, how it works, how it relates to us. At the point of having seen the complete picture of samsara, of having completely understood its mechanism, nirvana becomes redundant. In what is called the enlightened state, both samsara and nirvana are freed.

In order to see thought processes (sensations and perceptions that occur during the practice of samatha) as they are, a certain sense of openness and precision has to be developed. This precise study of what we are, what our make-up is, is closely related with the practice of tantra. In the tantric tradition it is said that the discovery of the *vajra body*—that is, the innate nature of vajra (indestructible being)—within one's physical system and within one's psychological system is the ultimate experience. In the samatha practice of the Hinayana tradition, there is also this element of looking for one's basic innate nature as it is, simply and precisely, without being concerned over the absence of "me" and "my."

From the basis of the samatha practice, the student next develops what is known as *vipassana* practice. This is the practice of insight, seeing clearly, seeing absolutely, precisely—transcendental insight. One begins to realize that spending one's whole time on the details of life, as in the samatha practice, does not work. It is still somehow an adolescent approach. It is necessary to begin to have a sense of the totality. This is an expansion process. It is parallel with the tantric practice of the mandala. Having started with what is called the *bija* mantra, the seed syllable in the middle of the mandala, there is then the expanding process of discovering the four quarters of the mandala. Working with the seed syllable has the samatha quality of precision, looking at the definite qualities of things as they are. Having established the seed syllable, one puts other symbols around it in the four quarters, one expands one's mandala. Similarly in the vipassana practice, having established the precision of details, one begins to experience the space around them. In other words, in making a pot, the importance is not so much on making the pot itself, but on shaping the space. Just so, in the vipassana practice the process is one of trying to feel the space around the pot. If one has a sense of the space one is going to create by producing a pot, one makes a good potter. But if one is purely concerned with making a shape out of clay without having a sense of the space, one does not make a good potter; or a good sculptor either, for that matter. In this way of beginning to relate with the space, vipassana is gradually letting go, a releasing and expanding.

From this point it is then possible to get a glimpse of the *shunyata* experience. The obstacle to the shunyata experience is the split between basic being and one's concept of it, between one's being and one's projections. All kinds of questions, problems and obstacles arise in relation to this division. The reason that the first glimpse of shunyata becomes possible at this point is that, having seen the details of things as they are through samatha practice and experienced the space around them through vipassana, one begins to relax. One begins to experience the needlessness of defending or asserting oneself. At this point shunyata emerges as the simple absence of those walls and barricades of defense and assertion. One begins to develop the clear and precise experience of seeing a tree as just a tree; not one's version of a tree, not a tree called such-and-such, but a tree just as it is. The culmination of the experiential process of the development of intellect is the experience of shunyata, which is the experience of the non-existence of duality. The research work is already accomplished, the process of searching for something has been laid to rest. This is the attainment of prajna.

From this point the intellect begins to turn towards *jnana* or intuition. Up until now the learning process has been regarded as receiving teaching; it has been an experimental course of study with the object of finding out who, what and where we are. In that sense the practices of both the Hinayana and Mahayana levels are a step towards the understanding of the mandala within the body, the mandala within consciousness and the mandala within the environmental situation of one's life. According to the tantric tradition, three levels of experience are always necessary—outer, inner and secret. The outer experience is relating with form; the inner experience is relating with the subtleties of form. The subtleties of form *are* the space, in the sense we have referred to of a pot and the space around it. The secret experience is that the form and the space are the same, that there is no difference between form and space.

On the level of the secret experience the subtleties are no longer an object of concern. If one keeps attending to the subtleties, then that itself becomes a veil—one is still relating to the situation as a learning process, rather than the actual process of experience. But it is not possible to arrive at the level of direct experience without going through the learning process of understanding scientifically. The practice of meditation in Buddhism begins with scientific research in which one learns to make friends with oneself and learns what one is. Having completely and thoroughly understood that, then one can expand into the further dimension of understanding which is the level of direct experience without any props.

CHAPTER FIVE

The Indivisibility of Openness and Compassion

I would like to discuss the implications of the following Sanskrit verse:

śūnyatākaruṇābhinnam bodhicittam iti smṛtam

"The indivisibility of *shunyata* and *karuna* is termed bodhicitta."

Here we have two terms which are of key significance in tantra, shunyata and karuna. The terms are not restricted to the tantric level, but appear fairly early on in the development of the Buddhist tradition. Shunyata was originally an elaboration of the concept of *anatman*. The meaning of anatman was that there is no abiding principle in things. Later on, shunyata became one of the central concepts of the Mahayana. For the student of tantra, it remains a sort of objective reference of which he must be aware in order to pursue his practice onto further levels of subtlety.

Shunyata is usually translated "emptiness" or "void." These translations are thoroughly misleading, because shunyata is a highly positive term. Unfortunately, the early translators were not very sophisticated and allowed themselves to be misled by the sense of shunya in ordinary everyday language. In this popular language, if a glass had no water in it, it could be called shunya. But this is not at all the sense of shunyata in Buddhist philosophy.

Shunyata can be explained in a very simple way. When we perceive, we usually attend to the delimited forms of objects. But these objects are perceived within a field. Attention can be directed either to the concrete, limited forms or to the field in which these forms are situated. In the shunyata experience, the attention is on the field rather than on its contents. By "contents," we mean here those forms which are the outstanding features of the field itself. We also might notice that when we have an idea before our mind, the territory, as it were, delimited by the idea is blurred; it fades into something which is quite open. This open dimension is the basic meaning of shunyata.

This openness is present in and actually presupposed by every determinate form. Every determinate entity evolves out of something indeterminate and to a certain extent also maintains its connection with this indeterminacy; it is never completely isolated from it. Because the determinate entity is not isolated from the indeterminacy and because nevertheless there is no bridge between the two, our attention can shift back and forth between one and the other.

The perception of shunyata as openness is connected with the development of what is known as *prajna*. Because there are some very fantastic translations in vogue of this term prajna, it is worthwhile having a good look at what the term means. There are various words in Sanskrit which refer to the cognitive process. Two most frequently used ones are prajna and jnana. If we look at the words, we immediately notice that both contain the root *jña,* which signifies the cognitive potentiality. Jnana is the primary formation from this root in the Sanskrit language; in prajna, the same root *jña* is there with the prefix *pra.*

If we look at the Tibetan translations for these terms, we find that the very same root connection has been preserved. The Tibetan for prajna is *shes-rab,* and for jnana it is *ye-shes.* In both cases the *shes,* the cognitive potentiality, is there. *Ye* means "primordial" or "original." Thus ye-shes refers to primordial awareness. The Sanskrit prefix *pra* and the Tibetan particle *rab* have the sense of "heightening" or "intensification." Therefore, shes-rab or prajna refers to an intensification or heightening of the cognitive processes. The cognitive potentiality that is present in everyone is to be developed, intensified, and brought to its highest pitch. To bring this potentiality to its highest pitch means to release it, to free it from all the extraneous material that has accumulated.

What does it mean to free something? In the Western world, freedom has usually been used as a negative term: we speak of freedom from this, freedom from that. The logical conclusion from this usage, a conclusion which nobody likes to draw, is that we must also reach the point of getting rid of freedom from freedom. It does not help to have recourse to the construction of "freedom-to," freedom to do this, freedom to be that. Freedom-to implies subordination to some transcendental hocus-pocus and that makes freedom disappear as quickly as the negative proposition does. We see, then, that freedom cannot be considered as a separate thing relative to something else. It must be itself an existential fact. In this sense, freedom is not something that has to be achieved—it is basic to everything.

Freedom is inherent in all the cognitive processes. Here it helps to see that the opposite of freedom is not determination but compulsion. One is quite free to determine one's way of life, free to determine whether to look at things in a categorical way or an aesthetic way. That is, we can look at things relative to a set of goals to be achieved, or can simply appreciate them, and recognize their intrinsic value. So we must understand that freedom is a basic phenomenon and not some end-product of getting rid of something or subjecting oneself to some transcendental nebulosity, as it would seem that Western philosophy has generally approached it.

Prajna or shes-rab as the heightening of the cognitive capacity, also means a weakening of the network of relative considerations in which, ordinarily, it is embedded. The weakening of this network permits the emergence of the cognitive capacity in its original freedom.

Prajna operates on different levels. It is operative when we listen to someone merely on a rudimentary level, when we merely hear something that the person we are listening to says. Just to hear what someone is saying, some understanding must be there. Prajna can be present on a more significant level. For instance, we can go beyond the mere momentary taking in of what someone says, to the point where we retain it and think about it. This may lead us to weigh seriously what we have heard and to try implementing our conclusions such that we embody them in our lives.

Prajna can operate on a still further level. Instead of attending to what we perceive, hear or think about, in terms of categories related to the narrow limits of self-preservation or personal ends, we can come to appreciate things as values in themselves. When we come to this point there is a sort of a release, since there is no longer a need to manipulate our perceptions—we can let things be as they are. In speaking of arriving at this point it is possible to speak of freedom as an achievement, but we must see that this freedom has been there all the time. However, we have lost sight of this freedom through being involved with all sorts of unnecessary constructions—constantly seeing things as means in relation to our personal orientation. Having come to this basic appreciation and openness, we have the possibility of staying with it and seeing things as valuable, or we can fall back to seeing things as means for further means *ad infinitum*.

It is at this crucial point that shunyata comes in. Shunyata is the objective correlate of this heightened or opened state of awareness. In this state, we do not see different things but we do see things differently. When I meet someone, I can immediately snap into a state of mind where I am asking myself what I have to gain or lose from meeting this person and I can then involve myself in the appropriate strategy. Or, I can merely take in the impression of this person and relate to him without preconception. Very likely if I do the latter, a very satisfactory meeting will ensue. I have related to this open dimension of my impression. Now this is a very simple thing, there is nothing special about it and anybody can do it. But, as I have said, the simplest things are often the most difficult. Probably one of the most difficult things is for a person to do without his fixations and preconceptions. They seem to provide so much security; yet a person who follows his fixations always suffers from a sense of lack or loss—as if something were missing.

When we speak of shunyata, we are speaking of the open dimension of being. We can be aware of this open dimension, but in order to perceive it our perceptive faculty must be open, without a bias of any kind. If our way of perceiving is tainted by any sort of predisposition or reservation, we are right then out of the openness. We have already narrowed our view, and this, in the end, will be quite unsatisfying.

We must be very careful not to regard openness as an entity. If we do that, we shall have made a concept of it, which automatically fixes it and makes it something definite. It is precisely this that we have had to break out of in order to perceive it. This is where past mistakes have been made in the history of Buddhism. Someone tried to say that prajna is shunyata. But prajna is not shunyata. Shunyata is the objective pole of prajna, the open quality of things which the cognitive process relates to when it reaches the level of true prajna.

We cannot predicate anything of prajna except to say that when it is properly prajna it must be as open as that which it perceives. In this sense we might say that subjective and objective poles, (prajna and shunyata) coincide. With this understanding, rather than saying that prajna is shunyata, we can try to describe the experience by saying that it has gone beyond the dualism of subject and object. But we must not get too carried away by these descriptions and lose sight of the fact that they are only trying to bring home to us this simple experience that any of us can relate to directly if we so wish. We are free to do it. It is up to us.

We have now seen that shunyata is always a reference of perception. All action is based on perception, since, naturally, we always act in the light of our awareness. This is true on every level. The less I am aware of another person, the less able I am to act appropriately in my relationship with him. We have the example of certain types of people with so-called "good intentions" who do not take the trouble to become aware of what the people they are being "good to" really need. They are so involved in their preconceptions and biases that they think whatever they like must be good for everybody. Such a person might like milk and exert himself to get everybody to drink milk. But what about people who are allergic to milk? Such a thought would never make any impact on such a person's good intentions. The example may appear ridiculous, but it is precisely this sort of ridiculous action that we encounter constantly in life. We act on the basis of our understanding, our awareness, and if this is not open and alive, then our actions are necessarily clumsy and inappropriate.

This leads us to the subject of *karuna*. It seems that awareness is not just there for the fun of the thing, but it implies action. Action carried out in the light of the awareness of shunyata, that is, the action of prajna, is karuna. Karuna is usually translated as "compassion" and in many cases that may be correct. But the word itself derives from the Sanskrit root *kr*, which denotes action. Just as with prajna, we can speak of karuna on many levels. On the highest level, on the level of the Buddha, we speak of *mahakaruna*, "the greatest karuna." Buddha's awareness was that of the awakened state of mind. He could not act otherwise than in the light of that complete awareness. This complete awareness is the fundamental example of the indivisibility of shunyata and karuna.

According to Buddhism there are three basic emotional complexes: passion-lust, aversion-hatred, and infatuation-bewilderment. These are named in terms of their ordinary or samsaric manifestations but they have latent possibilities of transformation. They are related to each other in a particular way. Bewilderment concerning the nature of what is going on can exist without entailing the extremes of passion or aversion. Passion or aversion, however, cannot come into play without the presence of basic bewilderment. Passion and aversion are emotional energies that have been distorted by an absence of precision which is this basic bewilderment.

Now in order to understand the nature of compassion, we can ask ourselves to which of these three basic emotional complexes compassion belongs. The usual response would be passion, since one ordinarily thinks that passion is related to love and love is not so different from compassion. But the Buddhist texts say the opposite: compassion belongs to hatred. The connection can be seen in the process that sometimes takes place when through enmity one person cuts another down and renders him helpless; then the one who has the power can aid the helpless one and feel himself a good person. This is the usual version of compassion and philanthropy.

But compassion is possible without aggression to create the original intimacy. On this level, the level of openness or shunyata, compassion is far more than the visceral emotion or sentimental urging that we ordinarily experience. On this level, we may speak of mahakaruna, which is based on the undistorted awareness of the awakened state of mind. There is a Sanskrit expression which runs as follows:

śūnyatākaruṇābhinnaṃ yatra cittam prabhāvyate
sā hi buddhasya dharmasya sanghasyāpi hi deśanā

"Where an attitude in which shunyata and karuna are indivisible is developed, there is the message of the Buddha, the Dharma, and the Sangha."

Where the mind is such that it is able to perceive the openness in being, then its action is consonant with this openness because it takes into account what is real. If, on the other hand, awareness is tainted, the mind will manifest in all the emotional forms which are distortions of the real.

Ordinarily a distinction is made between jnana and *klesha,* primordial awareness and distorted emotional mind. We see here that they are not two different things—the one is a distortion of the other. Because klesha is a distortion of jnana it can be, so to say, rectified and returned to its source. This comes as a result of the development of prajna which, when heightened, can cut through the potentiality for distortion. This was the emphasis of the *Prajnaparamita* literature. Through prajna a person is led out of the narrow confines of his fictions, led not into some realm beyond, but into the actual world that is right here. Again, the awareness of the awakened mind is not of some new realm of objects; we do not see different things, we see things differently.

When, through prajna, the point is reached where shunyata and karuna are indivisible, there emerges *bodhicitta* (the bodhi-mind). Bodhicitta is that in which all that has been a limit has fallen away and all the positive qualities of mind have become active. This active aspect of the bodhicitta is what is meant by karuna. On this level, karuna is compassion in the true sense of that word—*con-passio,* "to feel with." This means to feel with what is real. It goes with the recognition of what is real and valuable in itself, not by virtue of some assigned or projected value which is basically subjective in character.

We have such a strong tendency to approach our experience only as a possible confirmation of the conceptions we already have. If we are able to be open, we grow. If we seek to relate everything to our preconceptions, then we are narrowing ourselves, narrowing being and we become lifeless. If we fail to see the vividness of life and try to pigeonhole it, we ourselves become pigeonholed, trapped. We must attempt to relate to this innate capacity for openness that is there, this self-existing freedom. If we are aware in this way, we will act accordingly. If we see things as valuable in themselves, then we will act productively so that value is retained and augmented rather than destroyed and reduced.

If we constantly relate to and defend our preconceived ideas, everything is automatically reduced to what is known as *vikalpa,* concept, which means something that is cut off from the whole. Then we have just the fragmentary world in which we are usually involved.

The foundation of the creative approach is openness, shunyata. It is more than the "nothing," by which it is usually translated. According to Buddhist tradition, this openness is the basis on which we can enrich our lives. It is the basis of the various tantric practices.

CHAPTER SIX

The Development of Shunyata

WE have discussed the meditation practices of samatha and vipassana. The union of the samatha experience with the vipassana experience leads to a further meditation practice, known as *mahavipassana*. The mahavipassana practice corresponds to the birth of the shunyata experience. The intensive experience of form of samatha and the intensive experience of totality, total environment, of vipassana combine to give birth to the experience of shunyata. This experience produces a new dimension—one finds one doesn't have to defend oneself any longer. The experience of shunyata brings a sense of independence, a sense of freedom.

This is not a matter only of sitting meditation practice; daily living situations are very much a part of these experiences. The six transcendental qualities of a Bodhisattva—generosity, discipline, patience, exertion, meditation and prajna or transcendental knowledge—all these together contribute to the development of the shunyata experience.

The experience of shunyata is a by-product of the process of letting-go. This process consists in the application of the five transcendental qualities of a bodhisattva combined with the precision and clarity of prajna. The five qualities act as auxiliaries, which prajna directs. It is said that when the universal monarch goes to war he is accompanied by his army composed of five different kinds of forces—cavalry, elephant, chariots and so on. So the birth of shunyata takes place through the application of the skillful action of these five qualities with the guidance of prajna providing the basic strength.

Being related with these active characteristics, shunyata is clearly not a state of trance or an absorption of some kind. It is a fearless state. Because of this fearlessness, one can afford to be generous. One can afford to acknowledge a space which does not contain any conflicts of that and this or how and why. No questions of any kind exist at this point. But within this state there is a tremendous sense of freedom. It is an experience, I suppose one could say, of having gone beyond. But this does not mean that one has gone beyond in the sense of having abandoned "here" and therefore having gotten beyond to "there." Rather it's that one is here, or one is there, *already.*

So a tremendous sense of conviction begins to develop with the shunyata experience. Shunyata provides the basic inspiration for developing the ideal, so to speak, of bodhisattva-like behavior.

But there is a further level of experience beyond that of bodhisattva, which is that of a yogi. It has been said that ordinary people should not try to act as bodhisattvas, bodhisattvas as yogis, yogis as siddhas, and siddhas should not try to act as Buddhas. There are these different levels of experience. The shunyata experience corresponds to the level of a bodhisattva. But the shunyata experience is in a sense incomplete from the point of view of the next stage, which is the experience of *prabhasvara,* luminosity. Prabhasvara is the ultimate positive experience. Shunyata is like the sky. That space of the sky being there, it becomes possible for cosmic functions to take place within it. It becomes possible for there to develop sunrise and sunset. In the same way, within the space of shunyata, of openness and freedom, it becomes possible for students to begin to deal with the actual experiences of non-duality, rather than celebrating the achievement of non-duality. This is the prabhasvara experience, which is a way of acknowledging the Buddha-nature that exists within one. One is now so positive and so definite that one no longer has the fear that dualistic notions and ego-clingings might reinstate themselves.

Prabhasvara is another kind of space within which all kinds of perspectives of the positive quality of spiritual development present themselves. Finally actually realizing that one is impregnated with Buddha, one no longer has to look for external situations through which to create or build up enlightened experience. One acknowleges the enlightened being that is part of one's make-up, part of one's whole being.

From the prabhasvara experience, gradually a further development takes place, which leads to the *mahamudra* experience—still a further space. The space of mahamudra is even much more positive than that of prabhasvara. Frequently, explanations of mahamudra speak in terms of symbolism, since mudra means symbol. But on this level, symbols do not exist as such; the sense of experience ceases to exist. What one perceives is actual reality. That is why it is called *maha*mudra, the *great* symbol. It is the symbol born within, wisdom born within.

In Tibetan, this wisdom born within is referred to by the terms *ku* (sku) and *ye-she* (ye-shes). In this context ku means "body"—that aspect of the experience of the universe that is definite and solid, composed of forms. In the mahamudra experience forms become solid and definite forms, colors become bright and definite colors, sounds become definite sounds. Thought processes also become, in some sense, real, because at this point there is no longer any reason to condemn thoughts or try to mold them into a different pattern. It is just a spontaneous thinking of thoughts. Here spiritual development is not a matter of destroying anything but of rediscovering what is there through a process of unlearning preconceptions—constantly unlearning and unmasking. As a result of this constant unlearning, one begins to discover further details, further beauties in every area of one's being.

So ku, or body, is the direct experience of the living situation of the mandala spectrum, the whole range of life situations seen in terms of the mandala. And ye-she, or wisdom, has the same quality as ku—it is direct actual experience. It has nothing to do any longer with the spiritual learning process. It is complete and actual self-existing understanding.

The practice of mahamudra is to appreciate both positive and negative experiences as subtle symbolism, subtle expressions of basic being, to see the subtle basic situation, so to speak. The tantrism of mahamudra is very positive and spontaneous. Directly relating to the play of situations, energy develops through a movement of spontaneity that never becomes frivolous. The mahamudra experiences function naturally so that they lead us to destroy whatever needs to be destroyed and foster whatever needs to be fostered. The maturing process of mahamudra is one of extremely natural growth. One no longer has to try to struggle along the path. The notion of struggling along the path has dropped away at the level of shunyata.

Q: You say that having experienced shunyata, one no longer feels driven to struggle on the path?
R: Yes, that's right. You don't have to uncover any longer; you've uncovered already. At that point your innate nature begins to pick you up, and from then on spiritual development is a continually growing thing. It is as though you have reached the experience of the new moon; beyond that there is just a process of waxing. So the full moon begins to pick you up at the point of the shunyata experience.

Q: Could you say more about the difference between a yogi and a bodhisattva?
R: A yogi is one who has experienced the energy of the cosmos, the energy of the whole thing. He transmutes energies rather than trying to reform them, mold them into particular shapes. I wouldn't quite say the spirituality of the bodhisattva is molding energy into particular shapes, but still there is a constant note of gentleness in the bodhisattva practice, which suggests a subtle molding of some kind. The yogi's practice is more direct and rugged. Traditionally, the beginning of the yogi's practice is the understanding of symbolism, but not as symbolism. "Symbol" is really a rather inadequate word. The practice involves relating to the images that arise in living situations as decisive indications of one's psychological state. The bodhisattva experience has much less of this subtle

moment-to-moment insight. It is much more of a general lifestyle, a question of general behavior, rather than a continual relating to vivid details.

Q: Somehow it seems that this distinction between bodhisattva and yogi is artificial, like an article of religious dogma.
R: It's a progress. You begin as a bodhisattva, then you become a yogi. The dogma of religion drops away right at the beginning when you become a bodhisattva. As a yogi you pick up further on the non-dogmatic quality, but you also begin to enjoy the spiritual implication of things much more.

Q: Could you explain what you meant by the phrase "mandala spectrum"?
R: Actually, that's quite simple. At that stage you have developed very keen perception—sense of smell, of touch, of vision, of hearing—all these have developed to a very keen and acute level, a very precise level. We are speaking here of true perceptions, devoid of concepts. Nothing gets in the way. Having developed that ability, having entered this new dimension in which you are able to deal with situations directly, you see the world as it is; and this world-as-it-is becomes more and more complex. So many branches are branching out everywhere. At the same time, within this complex set-up of the world, simplicity presents itself as well: all these elements of the complexity branch out from one root, so to speak. The appreciation of this is the perception of the mandala spectrum. This appreciation, one might say, is curiosity in the fundamental sense—the actual, true curiosity; absolute curiosity. When you're absolutely curious about things, you lose yourself. You become completely part of the object. That's part of what is meant by letting-go.

CHAPTER SEVEN

The Guru-Disciple Relationship

ONE of the most important figures in the history of Indian and Tibetan Buddhism is Naropa. Unlike some others whose names figure in the lineages of Buddhist spiritual transmission, Naropa was certainly a historical figure. Naropa is part of the Kagyü lineage of Tibetan Buddhism, being with his teacher Tilopa and his disciple Marpa the spiritual founder of that order. He is also recognized and venerated by all the Tibetan schools as the exemplary disciple.

The relationship between guru and disciple is of tremendous importance in Buddhist spiritual transmission. The relationship is not merely a matter of historical interest; it continues as an important factor up to the present day. This relationship is based on trust. But before such trust can be developed, there must be a period during which the guru tests his disciple. This process of testing is seen in a very complete way in the trials and difficulties Naropa was put through by his teacher Tilopa. A long time passed before Tilopa was willing to impart his knowledge to his disciple.

The testing of a disciple by the guru is, in a way, quite simple. A student comes to a teacher and asks for instruction. The teacher might well say, "Well, I don't know very much. You'd better try some one else." This is an excellent way of beginning the testing. The student might well go away, which would be a sign that he is not really very serious.

Because of the intimacy of the relationship between teacher and disciple, whatever happens between the two is vital to the teacher as well as the disciple. If something goes wrong, it reflects on the teacher as well as the disciple. The teacher must know better than to accept a student who is not ready to receive the teaching he has to offer. That is why before giving instruction, he will test the readiness, willingness and capacity of the student to receive it. This means the student must become, to use the traditional image, a worthy vessel. And because of the intimacy of the prospective relationship, the student must also in his way test the teacher. He must scrutinize him to see if he is really able to transmit the teaching, if his actions tally with his words. If the conditions are not fulfilled on both sides the relationship is not worthy to be engaged.

The tradition of the guru-disciple relationship has been handed down from ancient times in India as we see from the texts. The Tibetans took over this practice from the Indians and to this very day they enact it in the traditional manner. This close relationship has not only the work of passing on the oral teachings, but also of preserving the continuity of personal example.

Naropa was a worthy vessel. He was willing to undergo every kind of hardship in order to receive teaching. His hardships began with his search for a teacher. Naropa spent years in his search. And this search was actually part of the teaching his teacher imparted to him. Before Naropa saw Tilopa in his own form, he encountered him in a succession of strange guises. He saw him as a leprous woman, a butcher, and in many other forms. All these forms were reflections of Naropa's own tendencies working within him, which prevented him from seeing Tilopa in his true nature, from seeing the true nature of the guru.

The term *guru* is an Indian word, which has now almost become part of the English language. Properly used, this term does not refer so much to a human person as to the object of a shift in attention which takes place from the human person who imparts the teaching to the teaching itself. The human person might more properly be called the *kalyanamitra*, or "spiritual friend." "Guru" has a more universal sense. The kalyanamitra is one who is able to impart spiritual guidance because he has been through the process himself. He understands the problem of the student, and why the student has come to him. He understands what guidance he needs and how to give it.

To begin with, spiritual guidance can only be imparted in the context of our physical existence by a person who shares with us the situation of physically existing in this world. So the teacher first appears in the form of the kalyanamitra. Then, gradually, as his teaching takes root within us and grows, its character changes and it comes to be reflected in the teacher himself. In this way an identification of the guru and the kalyanamitra takes place. But it is important that the guru be recognized and accepted as the guru and not confounded with the kalyanamitra in the manner of a mere personality cult. It is not a simple equation between the guru and the kalyanamitra. Still the kalyanamitra must be recognized as one able to give the knowledge which the student desires, which he needs, in fact, as a vital factor in his growth.

Here again we can refer to the example of Naropa. In the beginning, Naropa failed to understand the process in which he was involved. The inner growth that was already being prepared and taking root in him was still obscured by the many preconceptions he had. He continued to see the manifestations of his guru in the light of his ordinary conceptions, rather than understanding that they were symbols presenting the opportunity of breaking through preconceptions. These manifestations gave him the opportunity to be himself, rather than his idea of himself as a highly capable person.

We must remember that Naropa came from a royal family. His social prestige was great and he had become, in addition, a renowned pandit. And so in the process of trying to relate to his guru, his pride came into play. He felt that, as a person already renowned for his understanding, he should have all the answers already. But this was not the case. Only after the testing period did any real answers begin to emerge. This testing process actually effected the removal of his preconceptions. It was actually the teaching itself in the most concrete terms. No amount of words would have achieved the result that came about through his exposure to the rough treatment, the shock treatment, to which Tilopa subjected him. At the very moment in which he would think that at last he had understood, that at last these endless trials were over—at that very moment he would realize that he had again failed to see.

In the whole process of learning that is involved here, and one can say that the Buddhist way is a way of learning, there is a continual oscillation between success and failure. Sometimes things go smoothly. This is a fine thing; but it may also be a very great danger. We may become too self-sure, too confident that everything is going to come out as we would like it. Complacency builds up. So sometimes the failures that arise are very important in that they make us realize where we went wrong and give us a chance to start over again. Out of this experience of failure, we come to see things anew and afresh.

This oscillation between success and failure brings the sense of a way, a path; and here we touch upon the importance of the Buddhist tradition of the way. Buddhism has never claimed to be other than a way. The Buddha himself was only the teacher who showed other people the way which he himself had to travel, whatever the vicissitudes of success and failure. But it is always true that if a person fails, he can start again. If the person is intelligent, he will learn from the mistakes he has made. Then these mistakes will become ways of helping him along, as happened in the case of Naropa. Quite often Tilopa asked him to do things which were quite out of the question from Naropa's ordinary point of view, which quite went against the grain of his conventional frame of reference. But this was very much to the point. Conformity to the accepted way of looking at things would bring nothing. The point was to gain a new vision.

If we come to a new vision, a new way of looking at things, its mode of application may quite well be different from what is commonly accepted. This has always been the case with the great spiritual leaders of mankind, wherever we look. These people have broadened and widened our horizon. Through their action we have experienced the satisfaction of growing out of the narrowness of the ordinary world into which we happen to have been born.

When Naropa had shown that he was a person worthy of receiving instruction, the whole pattern we have been describing changed. Tilopa then showed himself the kindest person that could be imagined. He withheld nothing that Naropa wished of him. There is a Sanskrit expression, *acarya musti,* which means the "closed fist." This is an expression that has often been applied to gurus who withold the teaching. At a certain point, if the teacher withholds instruction, it is a sign that he is unsure of himself. But this was certainly not now the case with Tilopa. He gave everything that he had to his disciple.

This is the manner of continuing the teacher-disciple relationship. At a certain point the teacher transmits the entirety of his understanding to a disciple. But that the disciple must be worthy and brought to a state of complete receptivity is one of the messages of Naropa's life. And so, in his turn, Naropa led his disciple Marpa through the same preparatory process, and Marpa led his disciple Milarepa. Milarepa's biography tells us that Marpa had him build a house out of stone. He had hardly finished the house when Marpa told him to tear the house down and begin over again. This happened again and again. We need not ask ourselves whether this is a historical fact. The symbolic message is quite plain. Marpa asked him to do something and Milarepa reacted with pride, feeling that he could do it. Milarepa did it his way without waiting for the instruction. Naturally, the results were not satisfactory and there was no alternative but to have him tear it down and build again from the beginning.

Here we see another aspect of the guru-disciple relationship. The disciple must start at the beginning. And this comes almost inevitably as a blow to his pride, because he almost always feels that he understands something already. It is usually a very long time before this pride is broken down and real receptivity begins to develop.

CHAPTER EIGHT

Visualization

On the disc of the autumn moon, clear and pure, you place a seed syllable. The cool blue rays of the seed syllable emanate immense cooling compassion that radiates beyond the limits of sky or space. It fulfills the needs and desires of sentient beings, bringing basic warmth so that confusions may be clarified. Then from the seed syllable you create a Mahavairocana Buddha, white in color, with the features of an aristrocrat—an eight-year-old child with a beautiful, innocent, pure, powerful, royal gaze. He is dressed in the costume of a medieval king of India. He wears a glittering gold crown inlaid with wish-fulfilling jewels. Part of his long black hair floats over his shoulders and back; the rest is made into a topknot surmounted by a glittering blue diamond. He is seated crosslegged on the lunar disc with his hands in the meditation mudra holding a vajra carved from pure white crystal.

Now what are we going to do with *that*?

The picture is uncomplicated; at the same time it is immensely rich. There is a sense of dignity and also a sense of infanthood. There is a purity that is irritatingly pure, irritatingly cool. As we follow the description of Mahavairocana, perhaps his presence seems real in our minds. Such a being could actually exist: a royal prince, eight years of age, who was born from a seed syllable. One feels good just to think about such a being.

47

Mahavairocana is the central symbol in the first tantric yana, the *kriyayogayana*. He evokes the basic principle of kriyayoga—immaculateness, purity. He is visualized by the practitioner as part of his meditation.

In the kriyayogayana, since one has already discovered the transmutation of energy, discovered all-pervading delight, there is no room for impurity, no room for darkness. The reason is that there is no doubt. The rugged, confused, un-clean, impure elements of the struggle with samsara have been left far behind. Finally we are able to associate with that which is pure, clean, perfect, absolutely immaculate. At last we have managed to actualize *tathagatagarbha,* Buddha-nature. We have managed to visualize, to actualize, to formulate a most immaculate, pure, clean, beautiful, white, spotless principle.

There is a widespread misunderstanding of tantra, which sees tantra as pop art. People have heard that the tantric approach is to accept samsara fully. The idea has developed that therefore we are declaring everything—sexuality, aggres-sion, ignorance—as legitimate and pure; that we accept the crudeness as a big joke. "The crudeness is the fun." Therefore, the idea runs, we can jump into tantra by being crude and dirty: "Since we have to live with the crudeness, let's consider it beautiful." But visualizing Mahavairocana is far different from the gesture of stealing a "Rue Royale" streetsign in Paris and sticking it up on our wall. The whole idea of tantra is very different from joining a club formed by tantric teachers in which it has been agreed to regard the mess of confusion as something liveable and workable, to pretend that our pile of shit is nice, fresh, earthy soil that we are sitting on. This is a great misunderstanding.

The misunderstanding seems to be that tantra comes into being out of some kind of desperation; that since we cannot handle the confusion, we accept the convention of tantra as a saving grace. Then the shit of our confusion becomes pictorial, artistic—pop art. Supposedly tantra acknowledges this view eagerly and formally. But there is something very crude about this idea. If tantra merely acknowledged that samsara had to be put up with, without seeing the absolute purity and cleanness of it, tantra would be just another form of depres-sion, and devoid of compassion.

Actually, far from beginning by exalting crudeness, the

introduction to tantra is fantastically precise and pure, clean and artful. It could be said that the kriyayogayana is to the Vajrayana what the Yogacara approach, which underlies Zen, is to the Mahayana. There is a pronounced artful quality, a great appreciation of purity and cleanness.

Just as bodhisattvas embodying the magnificent vision of the Mahayana are good citizens, tantric yogis are also extremely good citizens. Tantric practitioners are the good mechanics in garages, who know the infinite details of the functioning of machines with clean and precise mind. Tantric practitioners are good artists, who paint good pictures that do not try to con one. Tantric practitioners are good lovers, who do not take advantage of their partners' energy and emotion, but make love precisely, accurately, purely. Tantric practitioners are good musicians, who do not fool around banging away at random, but play precisely, musically. Tantra is by no means to be associated with marginal lifestyles, Bohemianism, where one is intensely critical of convention and takes pride in being rugged and dirty.

The right understanding of tantra is crucial for the practice of visualization. One Nyingma teacher said that undertaking the practice of visualization is like going to bed with a pregnant tigress. She might get hungry in the middle of the night and decide to eat you. On the other hand, she might begin to nurse you, creating the furry warmth and texture of basic space. Certainly practicing visualization without the proper understanding is extremely destructive. A kriyayoga text, the *Vajramala,* says that the practitioner of wrong visualization, instead of attaining the complete openness of Vajrasattva attains, the complete egohood of Rudra, the ultimate spiritual ape. The tantric scriptures abound with warnings about wrong visualization.

Generally, wrong visualization takes the form of intensifying ordinary mental objects. One creates an image out of wishful thinking. For example, in the middle of one's meditation practice a sexual fantasy arises and one decides to carry it out in complete detail—stage one, stage two, stage three and so on. This same approach can apply to visualizations of tantric material. Even in visualizing Mahavairocana, a child sitting on a lunar disc, one might be recreating one's ego projection. The result is the ultimate ape: "I am Mahavairocana, I am one with him; let no one challenge this." There is a sense of the beast, a great powerful chest, the cosmic gorilla.

There is a precise attitude and understanding of visualization corresponding to each level of tantra—kriyayoga, upayoga, yoga, mahayoga, anuyoga and maha ati. The student's understanding evolves organically from one stage of tantra to the next. But for the student to arrive at any proper understanding of visualization at all, it is absolutely necessary to have gone through all the previous stages of the path. He has to have developed the Hinayana understanding of suffering, impermanence and egolessness and insight into the structure of ego. He must have attained the understanding on the Mahayana level of the shunyata principle and its application in the paramitas, the six transcendental actions of the bodhisattva. It is not necessary to have completely mastered all of these experiences, but the student must have had some glimpse of their significance. He has to have used up his mental gossip or at least taken out a corner of it. Their must be some sense of having trod on the path of Hinayana and Mahayana before embarking on the Tantrayana.

If one has done this, then rather than coming as a reinforcement of ego's deception, visualization will be inspired by a sense of hopelessness or, to say the same thing, egolessness. One can no longer deceive oneself. There is the despair of having lost one's territory; the carpet has been pulled out from under one's feet. One is suspended in nowhere or able at least to flash his non-existence, his egolessness. Only then can one visualize. This is extremely important.

According to tradition, one of the principal masters who brought the Vajrayana teachings to Tibet from India was Atisha Dipankara. Atisha prepared the ground for Vajrayana by teaching surrendering. In fact he was known as the "refuge" teacher because of the extent to which he emphasized taking refuge in the Buddha, the Dharma and the Sangha. Taking refuge in the Buddha, the Dharma and the Sangha is a process of surrendering. Tremendous emphasis was laid by Atisha on surrendering, giving, opening, not holding onto something.

People who live in New York City have very vivid and definite impressions of that city—the yellow cabs, the police cars, the street scene. Imagine, for example, trying to convey this to a Tibetan living in Lhasa. If you wanted to teach him about America starting with New York, you could say: "New York City goes like this. There are streets, skyscrapers, yellow cabs. Visualize all that. Pretend you are in it." You could expound Newyorkcityness on and on and on, explain it in the minutest detail; but he would have tremendous difficulty visualizing it, actually having the feeling of being in New York City. He would relate to New York City as being some kind of mystery land. There would be a sense of novelty.

Teaching Americans to visualize Mahavairocana is like teaching Tibetans to visualize New York City. Americans simply have not had that kind of experience. So how is it possible to bridge such a gap? Precisely by going through the three levels of Buddhist practice. Without the basic mindfulness practices and the development of awareness, there is no way at all of beginning the visualization practice of tantra.

It is through these fundamental practices that one can begin to see why such emphasis is placed on purity and cleanness, on the immaculate quality of the Mahavairocana visualization. Because of those preparatory experiences, the infant born from a seed syllable, sitting on the lunar disc, becomes impressive, highly impressive. This sambhogakaya Buddha becomes beautiful because one has developed the possibility of unbiased experience. One can relate directly, egolessly; then a principle arising out of this unbiased level of experience, Mahavairocana, for example, becomes fantastically expressive. This is complete purity, purity that never had to be washed. If one tried to produce this kind of purity by using Ajax to clean up one's dirty image, one would simply create a further mess. The purity of tantric experience is real beyond question. The practitioner does not have to think twice: "Is this really happening or am I imagining it." The experience beggars uncertainty.

Visualization is a prominent part of tantric practice. One identifies with various iconographical figures—sambhogakaya Buddhas, herukas, dakinis. This is done to develop vajra pride. Vajra pride is different from ordinary stupid pride. It is enlightened pride. You *do* have the potentialities of the deity; you are him already. The magic is not particularly in the visualization, but there is magic in your pride, your inspiration. You *are* Mahavairocana. You are absolutely clean, immaculate and pure. Therefore you can identify with your *own* purity, your purity rather than that of an external god who is pure, rather than some kind of foreign element coming into you. You are awakening yourself.

So tantra is not magic in the sense of conjuring or involving oneself in a myth. Tantra is the highest level of a process of personal evolution. It is the ultimate development of the logic that runs through the entire Buddhist path.

Kriyayoga places particular emphasis on mudras, or hand gestures, as well as on visualization. In these practices you are, in a sense, competing with the Buddhas and deities. You are making their hand gestures, behaving like them, trying to become one. But again, it is not really a question of trying, but of thinking that you *are* one. Vajra pride is the pride that you *are* Buddha.

That one *is* the deities, one *is* the Buddhas is a big point for beginners in tantra. The problem may arise that one does not think one actually is. So one thinks: "I am supposed to think that I am Samantabhadra Buddha, I am Mahavairocana. Therefore I had better crank myself into that role." This remote approach, instead of the directness of actually *being* that deity, is considered cowardice or stupidity. In order to develop vajra pride, one has to relate directly to the pain of situations, in this case the pain of actually being the deity, and see the value of it. Then that pride has something valid to be proud of.

It is in connection with the development of vajra pride that kriyayoga makes its strong emphasis on purity. You are spotlessly pure because there is no room for doubt. This is associated with the view of the phenomenal world in mahamudra. The phenomenal world is seen as completely colorful, precisely beautiful *as it is*, beyond acceptance and rejection, without any problems. You have seen things in this way because you have already cut through your conceptualized notion of a self and you have seen through its projections. Since that is the case, there is nothing that could come up that could be an obstacle in your handling the situation. It is totally precise and clear. *As it is*.

CHAPTER NINE

Empowerment and Initiations

I would like to speak about the initiations or *abhishekas,* to put them in proper perspective in terms of how they apply, when they come and what is meant by them. In order to understand this intricate pattern, we must have a picture of the whole gradual process of spiritual development in Buddhism.

The situation in which spiritual development takes place is represented visually in the Tantrayana as a mandala. A mandala is understood as a center which is beautiful because of its surroundings which are present with it. It represents a whole situation in graphic form. There is the center which stands for the teacher, or more esoterically, for the guru. The guru is never alone, but exists in relation to his surroundings. The surroundings are seen as the expression of a new orientation in relation to this center. The mandala is set up in terms of the four cardinal points of the compass. These points symbolize an orientation in which all aspects (directions) of the situation are seen in relation to the guru and therefore have their message. The whole situation becomes, then, a communication on the part of the guru or teacher. It depends on our level of spiritual growth whether we see the guru only concretely as a person or can also see him symbolically.

The mandala has a certain specific quality in that each situation is unique and cannot be repeated. Only similarities can obtain. The mandala also has its own time factor which

53

cannot be equated with the passage of time as we ordinarily understand it. It has a quality of simultaneity of all aspects which goes beyond our ordinary understanding of sequence. If properly understood, the mandala leads us back to seeing what the spiritual path is, back to the possibility of becoming more related to our own being without identifying it with this or that. Even the understanding embodied in the mandala is traditionally surrendered and offered up as a guard against reification.

The Buddhist path, which leads to seeing one's situation as a mandala, begins with taking refuge. We take refuge in the three jewels—the Buddha, the Dharma, the Sangha. This can happen on various levels. There is the ordinary physical level of just repeating the formula. But this also involves a process happening within us. Regarding this inner level, we have the instruction to take refuge in something which is abiding, something which can actually offer refuge. We can only take refuge in something certain; otherwise taking refuge would be a pure fiction and would not provide the security we want. So, on the inner level, taking refuge means surrendering to those forces of which we ourselves are, so to speak, the last transformation. These forces have, in a way, become frozen in us. Taking refuge thus means to commit ourselves to a process of unfreezing, so that life's energy, or whatever we want to call these forces that operate through us and somehow get blocked, can flow freely.

Beyond this, taking refuge can relate to still deeper layers, until we come to the point where the distinctions, differentiations, and separations that are introduced by our ordinary thinking no longer apply. At this level, when we speak of taking refuge in the three jewels, it means taking refuge in something which is unitary in character. We only speak in terms of three aspects in an effort to describe it.

So the first step in tantric discipline is to take refuge and understand it properly, not just as an outer performance which may in some way be beneficial, but as a ceremony that is meant to awaken the basic forces which are dormant within us. The ceremony can only be effective in this way if there is also present in us something known technically as an *attitude*. This means here an attitude we have developed which has as its aim to permit all that is within us to reach its fullest range of play.

There also comes into play something of a highly practical character which we might refer to as friendliness or compassion. This means taking account of the fact that the realm we are coming into contact with through taking refuge is a broader one than that in which we ordinarily operate. This automatically brings in a sense of openness.

The next step after taking refuge is training the mind. This does not mean intellectual training. It means seeing our very being in a different light. The movement has several stages. First, it is necessary to see our mental processes clearly. Then we will see that they must be cleansed of the presuppositions with which we ordinarily approach things. Then we must understand what the nature of this cleansing or purifying process is. The whole movement is one that goes deeper and deeper within, towards our hidden depths in which the energies are now being made to flow again.

The abhishekas in the Tantrayana are the further developments of what was begun by taking refuge. This can be understood as a process of purification, which allows us more and more to see our situation as a mandala of the guru. Purification means overcoming what are technically known as the various *Maras*. Maras are what we refer to in modern terminology as overevaluated ideas. They are a force of death that keeps us from growing. Overcoming them is part of the tantric discipline.

Of these Maras one of the main ones is the ideas we have about our body. We unconsciously form and analyze it to the point where we no longer relate to it as a living structure. Our ideas about it have no use—they are only a limitation of the potentiality that is there. But even this limiting construct is never separated from its living source. Seeing this is a development which leads us more and more into the presence of the guru.

We may look at the relationship with the guru in terms of external and internal aspects. We may even see that the guru has appeared to us in various forms. Taking this broader view of the nature of the guru, we understand that there is always someone who points us towards or challenges us into spiritual growth. The relationship with the guru is always there—this is the point of view of tantra.

The process of seeing our life more and more directly also involves demolishing our fortress of conceptions about ourselves and the world. In this process there is a need for the so-called initiations or abhishekas. Abhisheka is derived from a Sanskrit root which means "to anoint." Its symbology is taken from the traditional Indian ceremony of the investiture of a ruler. Investiture takes place through the conferring of a certain power. This idea of power is taken up in the Tibetan translation of abhisheka as *wangkur* (dbang-skur). *Wang* means something like "power", but not in the sense of power politics or domination. Wangkur is an *empowerment* in the sense that henceforth the person so invested is enabled to give the greatest scope to the forces operating within him, forces which are of a fundamentally wholesome nature.

The first or *jar empowerment* is connected with the observable fact we have been discussing, namely, that we are attached to the conception we have of our body. In the Western world we are conditioned to think that the mind is superior to the body—we look down on the body. Now this is very naive. If the body were such a debased thing, then people should be only too happy to have it mutilated or weakened. But nobody would submit voluntarily to such a process, which in itself means that the body is very valuable. Our body is a most important orientation point. Everything we do is related to our body. You are situated in relation to me in terms of my body and in no other way. To realize the creative potential of this embodiment purification must take place.

The image of the first empowerment is purification. Essentially it is a symbolic bathing. A gesture is made of pouring water from a jar over the person receiving the empowerment. This is actually quite close to the normal Indian way of bathing, in the absence of modern plumbing facilities. It seems to mean just getting rid of dirt, in this case the conceptual structure we have with regard to our bodies. But this cleansing is also a confirmation of power, because it means that henceforth we will make better and more appropriate use of our being-a-body. It means we are on the way to realization of the nirmanakaya, realization of embodiment as ultimately valuable. This means being alive in certain measured-out and limited circumstances to which we relate as the working basis of our creativity.

These empowerments or abhishekas are stages in a unitary process. Once what was implied by the first empowerment has come to its maturity in us, there is a second. In some way these stages are actually simultaneous, since all aspects of experience are interconnected. Nevertheless, we are obliged to take them one after another.

The second abhisheka, the *secret* or *mystery empowerment,* has to do with speech and language—our mode of communication. It has to do with communication not only externally (with others), but also with communication in our own inner world. We scarcely realize that mentally we are constantly acting out to ourselves our particular melodrama, our version of what is happening to us. And we actually talk to ourselves about it. So there are certain predispositions and neurotic patterns in our way of communicating. On the level of the second empowerment we work with this material. We have to come to another, a more wholesome level of communication. Talk can go on endlessly without communicating anything. Many people talk and talk and talk and never have anything to say. In fact, the general run of our mental life is on this level of empty chatter. We use words as tacks to pin things down and lose the open dimension of communication. Our use of words in this way kills the very thing that makes life worthwhile. And it reflects back on the physical level and reinforces our limited way of being on that level.

But communication can go on in quite a different way. It need not take place even through the normal verbal forms. This is where *mantra* comes in. Mantra is communication on quite another level than the ordinary. It opens the way to the manifestation of our inner strengths and at the same time it prevents our minds from going astray into the mode of empty talk. The second abhisheka is an empowerment to live on this superior level of communication.

Our presence involves not only our embodiment and an activity of communication, but also a pattern of thinking. Ordinarily we think in concepts, and certainly for the practical purposes of life we must use concepts. But, on the other hand, concepts are also images that we impose on things. Concepts are forms that we present to ourselves concerning the living forces that we are in order to give them a label. Our mental life then goes on in terms of these labels. Here we see that this way of limiting things in advance, so to speak, takes place on the thinking level as well.

What we have been looking at on all three levels of body, speech, and thinking is an interlocking pattern of limitation. If we live, as we ordinarily do, in this pattern of limitation, we are stuck in a situation in which everything tends to get narrower and narrower. We are trapped in a web of decreasing possibilities. We are in a world where we can talk about less than we can think of, and do less than we can talk about.

The process of spiritual growth is about unfreezing this situation. And what a tremendous experience when life can flow freely again; when the buds bloom forth, when the rivers break up and the waters come flowing through in all their purity. The abhishekas are an opening into a new dimension, which one ordinarily never experiences. Suddenly one is introduced to something of which one has never been aware. In such a situation there is a great danger that the experience may be misunderstood. There will be a strong tendency to reduce it to our habitual frame of reference. If this happens, the experience can be quite harmful, especially in the case of the third abhisheka, on the level of thought.

Whether the third abhisheka is properly understood or not depends very much on the accurate interpretation of the symbols that come into play at this point. These symbols are the *karmamudra, jnanamudra, mahamudra,* and *samayamudra.* The functioning of the process of spiritual growth depends on our seeing them in another mode than our ordinary one.

The term *mudra,* literally translated, means "seal." But what is a seal? It is something that makes a very deep impression on what it comes in contact with. So it might be better to understand mudra in this context as a tremendous encounter in which two forces come together and make a very deep impression.

Karma comes from the Sanskrit root meaning "action," what one does in encountering the world. Usually, our major encounters are with other people; and people are both male and

female. Symbolically, the most potent form is our encounter
with the opposite sex. Now we can look at this situation
reductively and literally and think, in encountering a person
of the opposite sex, of taking the other person as a kind of
utensil. In that way we reduce the encounter to a very dead
item. True, sex is fun, but if it continues very long we get
bored with it. Here we have to understand the encounter on an
entirely different level than the one usually seen. A characteristic of the sexual encounter is that we are never at rest;
there is constant action and reaction. This by its very nature
can create an opening of awareness beyond the normal level.
An expanded awareness tinged with delight can arise.

If we have perceived the *karmamudra* in this constructive
way, rather than reductively, there is automatically a tendency to go further in the direction of open awareness. This
leads to the relationship with the *jnanamudra*. Suddenly the
whole picture has changed. The relationship is no longer
merely on the physical level, but there is an image involved
here, a visualization which mediates a complete degree of
appreciation and understanding. This opens up entirely new
vistas.

The inspirational quality is much stronger and more far-
reaching than with the karmamudra. We can reach a very
profound level of awareness in which we become fused with
the partner in a unitary experience. The distinction between
oneself and the other simply no longer holds. There is a sense
of tremendous immediacy, which also brings a sense of great
power. Again there is a danger of taking the experience
reductively and thinking that "Now I have achieved great
power." But if we are able to relate to this moment as an open
experience, we are then at the level of *mahamudra* or, in this
context, the greatest encounter.

When we have had this peak experience, we wish to retain it
or at least to make it manifest to ourselves again. This is done
through the *samayamudra*. The samayamudra involves the
various figures we see represented in the Tibetan thangkas or
scroll paintings. These forms are expressions of the deep
impressions that have come out of the encounters we have had
with the forces working within us. It is not as though we were,
so to speak, containers of these forces—rather, we are like

partial manifestations of them. In these encounters our sepa-
rateness and secludedness are momentarily abolished. At the
same time, our deadening reductive tendencies are overcome.
In the samayamudra we commit ourselves to the implications
of this great experience of openness through the symbology of
the tantric path.

After the abhishekas relevant to body, speech and thought,
there is still a fourth. As I have pointed out, these stages are
part of a unitary situation which we approach sequentially
only because of the limitations of our mode of experience. But
it is much more sensible to see them as a part of a great tableau
in which all the aspects are interrelated and fuse with one
another. It is on the level of the fourth abhisheka that we see
the previous experiences as aspects of a totality. These experiences fuse into an integrated pattern which cannot be destroyed. Through the empowerment their indivisibility is
clearly established.

At this point we cannot quite say that we have become one,
because even the idea of unity or oneness now no longer
applies. The term one is only meaningful if we have a two or a
three. Unity implies plurality as something else. But what we
are dealing with here is a unity which includes plurality.
Unity and plurality only seem contradictory when we con-
ceive of them as isolated terms. There can never be isolation
when everything is part of the whole pattern. Isolation is an
abstraction, but plurality is whatever we happen to find in the
world wherever we are. Not disrupting the unitary quality by
isolating units is the basic meaning of unity. And this comes
here as a deep inner experience.

This deep inner experience is the guru operating, and
through such profound experiences he has his tremendous
influence on the pattern of our spiritual growth. For in the
ultimate sense, the guru is none other than the Buddha—not
the historical Buddha but Buddhahood itself. In this way all
the empowerments are developments of the *guruyoga*. In the
guruyoga we attempt to come closer to our basic nature
through coming closer to the guru. In the empowerments we
are actually in connection with him. We are also in connection
with his lineage, those who have preceded him in the direct

transmission of the teaching and in connection with whom he remains.

Like the refuge formula and the empowerment ceremonies, the guruyoga practice has an outward form betokening a deeper experience. In this case the outward form is a kind of litany. But if, in reciting this litany, there is awareness of where in us these words come from, they follow back to the person whom we have chosen as our spiritual guide. The litany itself is not the ultimate thing, but it involves us in the fact that throughout human history there have been persons who have awakened. The presence of their example challenges us to look into ourselves and awaken to our own being. And in the process of coming closer to what is meant by their example, the nature of the guru as we relate to him again changes and becomes deeper. It increasingly reveals itself as a principle which is much more attuned to the real than our habitual sham.

The various ceremonies—the refuge, the guruyoga, and the empowerments are all established in an outward form so as to be repeatable. But it is of the greatest importance to be aware of the highly symbolical character of tantra as expressed in these forms. We must distinguish between a symbol and a sign. A sign can be put on anything and acts as an identification tag. A symbol always points beyond itself. It is only a pointer to, in this case, what cannot be said.

A great deal of harm has been done by abusing the repeatable character of these rituals and using the texts indiscriminately, without being aware of the different levels of the symbology. Only when a person has grown up to the point where he no longer confuses a symbol with a sign does he begin to come into real contact with the guru. Only then does the pattern of development available in the tantric tradition, beginning with taking refuge and leading through the various traditional practices and the four empowerments, have the effect of awakening the power that is within us. It makes us more and more alive and brings us to a new perception of our situation in which we see that we are never alone, never isolated ends-in-ourselves.

We see that we are always in a force-field, so to speak, in

which every act of ours has its effect on others and the whole field constantly has its effect on us. The empowerments introduce us progressively into the dimension of this vision. Once we have glimpsed it, the guru is always present, although he may not be clearly perceived. When one's vision begins to mature, one perceives the guru as the great challenger in the quest to be true to oneself.

CHAPTER TEN

Questions and Answers: Guenther

Q: Can you say something about mantra?

G: The word *mantra* comes from the noun *manas* and the verbal root *tra* ("to protect") according to the Indian explanation. The full explanation runs as follows:

manastrāṇabhūtatvād mantram ity ucyate

"Since it has become a protection of mind it is called mantra." Mantra is usually associated with certain syllables or combinations of syllables. It is completely wrong to try to read a meaning into these syllables as with ordinary words. This goes exactly counter to the purpose of mantra, which is to protect the mind from straying away into habitual fictions. These fictions are very much tied up with words. The function of mantra is to preclude the tendency of the mind to, so to speak, flow downward. We are forced here to use this spatial metaphor; we might also speak of the tendency of the mind to glide off into something, or to fall.

We encounter this same metaphor in Western religious thought, where it is said that man is a fallen being. Our mental process tends always to run to the lowest level, just like water. With water rushing downwards, once it has reached the bottom, it has lost its potential and there is practically nothing more that can be done. Well, it works the same way with our minds, going off into this system of fictions we have developed.

To give an example of mantra, I might use the word "love."
This word can be used in an everyday way so that it is
meaningless or in a way that renders it full of meaning. In the
latter case, it keeps something alive; in the former it's just a
piece of dead language. When a young man is courting a girl, he
may say "I love you" or address her as "my love." So saying, he
expresses something that no other word could better convey.
Some time later the couple goes to the divorce court, and he
says, "Well, my love, let us separate." In one case, the word
"love" is a mantra; in the other case, it's just an ordinary figure
of speech. So there is nothing mysterious about mantras.

Q: Dr. Guenther, could you give an idea of the sense of the
word *svabhava* in svabhavikakaya; it seems to be different than
elsewhere.
G: In the term *svabhavikakaya, kaya* is derived from the other
terms (dharmakaya, sambhogakaya, nirmanakaya). Then in
order to emphasize that existentially kaya is not dependent
upon anything else, you say svabhava. Here svabhava has a
sense something like "self-existing." The svabhavikakaya is
not different therefore from the dharmakaya, being that which
is not existentially dependent on anything else. The nirmanakaya and sambhogakaya are, however, dependent on the
dharmakaya.

Q: So it could not be said that the svabhavikakaya is dependent on the dharmakaya.
G: That's right. The term svabhavikakaya obviously evolved
in the clarification of what was meant by dharmakaya. Dharmakaya had two meanings. On the one hand, there is the usual
sense in which it is associated with the very nature of
Buddhahood. On the other hand, it also meant the sum total of
all the entities of reality. The latter sense is the early
Hinayana view of dharmakaya. This is still the meaning it has
as late as in the Hua Yen or Avatamsaka school. In later
Mahayana Buddhism the two senses always go together. Even
though they are both dharmakaya, there cannot be two dhar-
makayas. So we say that the absolute is dharmakaya and that
all things, seen as constituting and representing the absolute
are also dharmakaya. This insight presenting the rapproche-

ment of these two senses of dharmakaya was a contribution of the *Avatamsaka Sutra*. This sutra, incidentally, has never been found in any Sanskrit version.

Q: Can you explain sambhogakaya?

G: *Kaya* refers to the existential fact of being and *sambhoga* to being in communication with dharmakaya. The sambhogakaya is between the dharmakaya and the nirmanakaya. It is dependent upon and in communion with the dharmakaya. It is the level on which, as it is said, the teaching of the Buddha goes on uninterruptedly in that the person tuned in to this level always hears the Dharma taught. This is, of course, a figurative way of speaking.

Then from the sambhogakaya there is a further condensation which is the nirmanakaya, in which what was seen or felt on the sambhogakaya level is now made more concrete. *Nirmana* means "to measure out." On this level, the whole thing is put into a limited framework, which is understandable to us because, of course, our mind works within limitations.

Q: You've spoken quite a bit about the Yogacara. What about the role of the Madhyamika in the development of tantra?

G: The philosophical systems that developed in Buddhist India, the Vaibhashikas, the Sautrantikas and the Yogacaras (the mentalistic trends), were all lumped together in the traditional Tibetan surveys as reductive philosophies. They all try to subsume the whole of reality under particular existents, one under a particular existent of a physical kind, another under a particular existent called "mind." But in all cases they are reductive systems. Not to say that there wasn't a progress in the development of these systems.

The earliest, the Vaibhashikas, assumed mind and mental events, *citta* and *caitta*. Wherever there is mind there are also mental events. The Sautrantikas challenged this, showing that the mind *is* the mental events, so that there was no reason for this double principle. So they simplified it to saying a cognitive event was just mind. Still the Sautrantikas continued to speak of external objects corresponding to the objective pole of our cognitive experience, even though they regarded these external objects as only hypothetical causes of our cognitive experience. But further investigation showed that there was very little reason for assuming realities outside our experiencing of them. The realist formula would be $x = x + n$, where x is mind or experience and n is external realities. Now this is a nonsensical formula unless $n = 0$, which the realist will not accept. So if we analyze the situation in this mathematical form the realist hasn't got a leg to stand on.

The uncertainty over the status of n (external reality) had already been initiated by the Sautrantikas. Then the Yogacarcas drew the logical conclusion that there is only x, which *appears* as $x + n$. In reducing the whole epistemological formula to mind or experience alone, the Yogacaras still held on to this x. This is exactly what the Madhyamika critique of the Yogacaras undermined, showing, in effect, that holding to the principle of mind was still reducing reality to some particular existent.

So, for the subsequent development of tantra, the Yogacaras and Madhyamikas were of equal importance. The Yogacaras with their principle of mind provided something to deal with. After all, you must have something in hand to deal with. The Madhyamikas contributed the insight that one cannot believe in this what-you-have-in-hand as an ultimate answer. This criticism of the reductionist tendency which had characterized all previous Buddhist philosophy was a very important one indeed.

Q: Is dharmadhatu in the Vajrayana connected with the skandhas?
G: The skandhas are subdivisions of the dharmadhatu. This has always been accepted by all schools. Since the earliest times there has never been the slightest disagreement over the division that was made into the skandhas, the dhatus and the ayatanas, all of which together compose the dharmadhatu. The schools differed only over the logical status of these elements.

The earliest classification was made by the Vaibhashikas in the *Abhidharmakosha*. All the following schools adopted this classification. Even the Yogacaras, who would accept only mind as ultimate took it up; in fact they divided it up even more intricately than their predecessors.

As the first to attempt a systematization of what had been given by Buddha in the sutras, the Vaibhashikas based themselves on the Abhidharmapitaka, which itself originated from certain word lists. These word lists seem to have come about when, after the Buddha had died, his followers wanted to set up some kind of easy reference to the body of his teachings. It was to be something like an index. This began as word lists, almost like sets of synonyms and antonyms. In this way Buddha's followers began to organize the teaching. They would approach the whole of reality from the point of view of a single category they had under examination.

For instance, considering impermanence they noted that there were certain things that were impermanent and other phenomena to which the term impermanence did not apply. Thus they came to make a great division between that which is impermanent and that which is permanent. Everything in the transitory category were particular existents, divided into physical, mental, and others which were neither physical nor mental. Particular existents which were neither physical nor mental were, for example, attainment, aging or letters. Words are made up of letters—are these letters physical or mental? On the permanent side of this great division of reality was *akasha,* usually translated as space. We must be clear that in Buddhist philosophy the notion of space never indicates mathematical or locational space. It is more like lifespace or lived space. This space is irreducible and not transitory; it is there as long as one is alive (and after that one can enunciate no philosophical theories).

This great division into permanent and impermanent was adopted by later schools, but the way of looking at it was subject to continual criticism and revision. Vasubandhu, for instance, criticized some of the earlier statements from the Sautrantika point of view. Some of the criticisms were quite simple and purely linguistic. The Vaibhashikas had said, "The eye sees." This seems legitimate; probably none of us can find any reason to object to such a formulation. But the Sautrantikas said, "No, *we* see *with* our eyes." The Sautrantikas began criticizing the Vaibhashikas in this manner.

Eventually they wanted to know exactly what was meant by what they themselves were saying. This led them into a thorough analysis of perception. They became quite involved in what differentiated veridical from delusive perceptual situations. What could the criteria be? They found that the inquiry can be shifted from one level of absoluteness-relativity to another and that what was veridical on one level might be delusive on another. In this way the epistemological inquiry was greatly expanded. The Sautrantikas tried to keep their criteria consonant with common sense; but in the analysis of perception common sense is not a very reliable touchstone. Thus there was room for the Yogacaras to come in, make their critique and draw their conclusions.

But the Yogacaras' view, for all its sophistication in relation to the earlier schools, remained naive. In dealing with mind, they concretized and affirmed it as a particular existent. The odd thing is that when we make positive statements, we exclude. If we want to be inclusive, we must make negative statements; we must continuously say "not this, not that." If I say "horse," I exclude everything that isn't a horse. But certainly there are also cows. So in affirming as ultimate a particular existent we fall into this trap. This is precisely the point at which the idea of shunyata as openness enters. Shunyata is an absolutely positive term in a negative form.

Q: Could you give an idea of the significance of *dakini*?
G: The Tibetan word is *khandroma* (mkha'-'gro-ma). Literally it means "walking over space." Again here space, akasha, refers not to mathematical or locational space but to lifespace. "Walking over" signifies a kind of appreciation. This appreciation of space is inspiration which is depicted symbolically in female form. This inspiration is the *dakini*; it is the inspiration of the openness of the space. The rich symbolism of the dance of the dakinis indicates that the inspiration of openness comes not in one form but in many. This dance, a series of graceful movements, also expresses the fact that each moment is a new situation. The pattern changes constantly and each moment presents a new occasion for appreciation, a new sense of significance.

Q: What is *lalita*?
G: Lalita is the graceful movement of the dance. There is never a state of rest. Lalita also has a strong connotation of beauty. Beauty here is not different from the valuable; and the valuable is not different from what is. When we try to catch it or grasp it, it is destroyed.

Q: It has been said that the Hindu and Buddhist tantras arose simultaneously, that one did not precede the other. Do you think that is accurate?

G: I think that is correct, yes. They are quite different and probably one could not be derived from the other. The emphasis in the Hindu tantra is on a way of doing, creating. The Buddhist tantra with its theory of prajna,appreciative discrimination, having equal status with upaya, action, has quite a different emphasis. For one thing, the Hindu term *shakti* never appears in Buddhist texts. Those who say it does can never have seen the actual texts. But the idea of shakti is of paramount importance in the Hindu tantra.

The Hindu tantra took over the Samkhya system of philosophy, which is based on the dualism of *purusha,* the male factor, and *prakrti,* the female or shakti factor. Purusha is usually translated as "pure mind" and prakrti as "matter." This is not to be understood in terms of the Western division between mind and matter. Mind and matter as conceived of in the West are both in the prakrti. Purusha is a fairly useless term; the concept corresponding to it fits nicely into a male dominance psychology. The purusha, according to the Samkhya system, throws its light on the prakrti, and this starts a process of evolution.

There are some definite difficulties in this conception. The purusha is defined as being everpresent. If this is the case, liberation can never take place—the everpresence of the purusha means that he throws his light, irritates the prakrti, continuously. Since there is this dominance of the male over the female and at the same time everything takes place within the prakrti—all cognition, all action, everything—the system is logically untenable.

Still it has certain good points. The analysis of the prakrti into the three strands or *gunas—sattvas, tamas, rajas—*can account well for the psychological differences in individuals. Some people are more intelligent, lazy, temperamental than others. This is well accounted for. Metaphysically, however, the system is complete nonsense. It cannot do what it sets out to do, which is provide for the possibility of liberation. It says if a separation between purusha and prakrti takes place there is liberation; but this is impossible if the purusha is everpresent. This was later understood by the followers of the yoga system of Patanjali. They tried to get out of the difficulty by postulating a super-purusha, an *ishvara,* a god. But this merely opens the way to an infinite regress. If one is not enough and a second is supposed to be, why not a third, a fourth, a fifth?

Such a set of improbable conceived principles was bound to present such difficulties. The prakrti is said to be unintelligent, but all intelligent processes occur in it. The purusha is said to be pure intelligence, but it doesn't cognize. This is like saying, "Look, I have a very special book; but this book has no pages, no print, no binding, no cover—but it is a book!"

Q: What is the movement of this relationship between purusha and prakrti supposed to be and how is it supposed to come to an end?
G: The prakrti or shakti is utilized by the purusha. The simile is that he asks her to dance and to perform various antics. Then he says, "Now I am fed up with this so stop it." Then he says, "Now we are free." This is a bit primitive.

Q: It is true that the Buddha's actual words were never recorded?
G: Yes.

Q: Would you be able to say anything, then, about how the sutras came about?
G: After the Buddha died an effort was made to collect what the Buddha had said. But all the sutras begin with the form, "Thus have I heard. . . ." Certainly there must be passages that were remembered correctly, but there are no means of verifying where the texts represent exact words, because none of the material was reported as direct quotation.

Q: It seems they could never have been the exact words, then.
G: The tremendous capacity for memory that existed in Eastern culture could counteract the likelihood that all the exact words were lost. The time when they codified and wrote down the Buddha' teaching was not necessarily the beginning of its preservation. It might have been decided at that point that it was a good idea to write it all down because the oral tradition *might* become disturbed. But up until that point the

oral tradition can be said to have been highly exact. Since the words were rehearsed after the death of the Buddha, this is not very doubtful. The words were precious at that point since the Buddha himself was no longer there. It is true that, whereas in some passages the reciter might give the exact words, in other parts he might recite only as he had understood. But this became accepted.

Another point is that the Pali sutras do not contain everything that was preserved in the tradition. The Sanskrit version preserved in the *agamas* has sections that were left out in the Pali. The Theravada canon definitely reflects a vested interest.

Q: What would you say is the basic point in the Buddhist view?

G: One basic thing that must be learned is what is meant by the I or the ego. We must understand this because the ego is the great stumbling block, a kind of frozenness in our being, which hinders us from any authentic being. Traditionally, the Buddhists ask what such an entity could consist of. Is it what we would call our physical aspect? Our feelings, motivations, our thought processes? These are the things we try to identify as ourselves, as "I." But there are many things that can be pointed out with regard to each one of these identifications to show that it is spurious.

The word "I" has very special peculiarities. We generally assume that this word is like any other; but actually it is unique in that the noise "I" can only issue in a way that makes sense from a person who uses it signifying himself. It has a peculiar groundless quality. "I" cannot apply to anything other than this act of signifying. There is no ontological object which corresponds to it. Nevertheless, philosophies, Oriental as well as Western, have continually fallen into the trap of assuming there is something corresponding to it, just as there is to the word "table." But the word "I" is quite different from other nouns and pronouns. It can never refer to anyone but the subject. It is actually a shortcut term which refers to a complicated system of interlocking forces, which can be identified and separated, but which we should not identify with.

To undermine the naive persistence of the ego notion is one of the first steps in Buddhism, a prerequisite for all further study. Furthermore, we have to see that the various aspects of ourselves that we tend to identify with from moment to moment as "I"—the mind, the heart, the body—are only abstractions from a unitary process. Getting this back into perspective is also a basic step. Once these steps have been taken, a foundation is laid; although in fact for a very long time we must continue to fall back into spurious identification.

This identification also has its objective pole. When we perceive something, we automatically believe that there is something real corresponding to the perception. But if we analyze what is going on when we perceive something, we learn that the actual case is quite different. What is actually given in the perceptual situation are constitutive elements of an object. For example, we perceive a certain colored patch and we say we have a tablecloth. This tablecloth is what is called the epistemological object. But automatically we believe that we have not only an epistemological object, an object for our knowledge, but also an ontological object corresponding to it, which we believe to be an actual constitutive element of being.

But then, on the other hand, we have certain other perceptions, and we say, "Oh, well, there is certainly nothing like this." If some one has delirium tremens and he sees pink rats, we certainly say there are no pink rats. But here he goes ahead anyhow and tries to catch them—and he behaves towards them as we do towards ordinary objects. In a certain sense, from the Buddhist point of view, we are constantly chasing about trying to catch pink rats. So here the question arises: if one perception is adjudged delusive and the other veridical, what could be the criterion used to make the distinction? All that can be said is that any object before the mind is an object in the mind. Any belief in ontologically authentic objects is based on an assumption which cannot withstand critical analysis.

What we have, then is a phenomenon which appears as having some reference beyond itself. But our analysis has shown us that this reference is only an apparent one on which we cannot rely as valid. Now this analysis is extremely valuable because it brings us back to our immediate experience, before it is split into subjective and objective poles. There is a strong tendency at this point to objectify this immediate experience and say that this fundamental and unassailable thing we have got back to is the mind. But there is absolutely no reason to posit such an entity as the mind; moreover, postulating this entity again shifts the attention out of the immediacy of experience back onto a hypothetical level. It puts us back into the same old concatenation of fictions that we were trying to get away from.

So there is a constant analysis, a constant observation that must go on, applied to all phases of our experience, to bring us back to this complete immediacy. This immediacy is the most potent creative field that can exist. The creative potential of this field is referred to in the tantric texts as *bindu*, or in Tibetan, *thig-le*.

Q: Is it possible, if one already has a certain experience of life, to start directly on the tantric path?
G: There's a certain danger involved in trying to do advanced practices without having the proper foundation. Unless one has actually gone through the preliminary experiences, conclusions may be drawn on the basis of insufficient information. And they may produce just the opposite effect of the one which is intended. Throughout Buddhist history there has been an emphasis placed on learning, learning more from the philosophical point of view. And this begins with seeing.

In traditional Buddhism what is usually learned at the beginning is the Four Noble Truths. But even these basic truths are the product of a long, long process gone through by the Buddha. It was after Buddha had already gone through all the traditionally accepted practices that the moment came which made him the Enlightened One. It was only after this moment that he formulated these four truths.

The Buddha formulated these truths in the inverse order of cause and effect. Usually we think in terms of cause then effect, but these truths are presented here in the order of effect then cause.

This order of presentation is educationally oriented. First we have to be brought face to face with what is there. Then, when we are willing to accept this, we can ask how it comes about. The third Dalai Lama wrote a very beautiful book on the stages of the spiritual path in which he uses an excellent simile to illustrate the nature of this learning process. A man is walking along, very contentedly, complacently, happily. He hasn't got a worry in the world. Suddenly there comes a great shock and he finds he has been hit by a torrent of cold water. This really gives him a jolt, and he looks right away to see what has happened. Having been brought face to face with a certain situation, his intelligence is entirely aroused. And he sees: "Oh yes, the waterpipe broke!" So he has seen the effect, determined the cause, and already he is at the point of the third truth—that there is a way to stop this. The third Dalai Lama goes on to apply this analogy on a much profounder level. First we must see what is there. In order to do this we need constant study. When we have really learned something about it, we automatically come to the point of beginning to practice in relation to what we have learned. There is a long process between my deciding I must be kind to others and the point where I actually am kind to others. Before such kindness becomes a part of us, we must learn a great deal about what there is.

In English there is the saying, "to see eye to eye." But perhaps more indicative of the actual attitude that exists in the West as the accumulated result of our tradition would be the saying, "to see I to I." Even if we had the tantric practices, they would be completely useless as long as we maintained this ego-oriented attitude.

In the tantric tradition we have the description of the experience of a brilliant light. It is a sort of formless energy which appears to us as a brilliant light. Now we cannot have this experience of light as long as we are involved with our ego's escaping the darkness. In fact it is this very ego involvement which blocks the light. So to begin with we must find out about this "I" which enters into and distorts our being. When we have understood what this is and how it has come about, then we can set those energies free which lead to transformation. The transformation to selflessness does not make us merely an amorphous entity, but leads directly to what the late Abraham Maslow called the "peak experience." Maslow also coined the term "plateau experience," which can be understood as the continuous extension of the peak experience. I think the plateau experience could be equated with Buddhahood, while recurrent peak experiences could be associated with the bodhisattva or arhat.

But as Maslow also pointed out, before we reach these experiences, there is a lot of work to be done. A solid foundation must be laid; otherwise any extraordinary experience we have will be extremely precarious and without ground and the next blast of wind will simply blow it away. We will be right back where we were, except worse off because the rubble of this extraordinary experience will now be in the way. So although there is a great tendency to try some shortcut, unfortunately it simply does not work.

Q: Is the concept of the alayavijnana somewhat analogous to Jung's idea of archetypes as potential roots of death, decay and rebirth?

G: It is close in some ways, but one should not directly equate the two. Jung comes quite close with certain of the archetypes, but being in the Western tradition, he falls into the idea that there is a someone, an entity, to whom the archetypes are related. This is where Jung was tied down by his Aristotelianism. I do not mean to demean Aristotelianism—after all, it is one of the finest systems produced by Western thought—but it definitely has its shortcomings.

To be more precise, Aristotle spoke of the psyche as an object of investigation. With this approach, we are already in a framework which presumes the division between subject and object. In this framework subject and object, rather than being complementary, different aspects of the same unity, are separate entities which are opposed to each other. The word "object" means "thrown against." The Indian terms do not have this dualistic character. The Indians spoke of the "apprehendable" and the "apprehender," which are very much on the same level, aspects of the same process. There cannot be one without the other.

Q: Is the process described through which the original split between the transcendental ego and the empirical ego takes place?

G: To try to put it on the level of ordinary experience, it seems to be similar to the process in which a person, feeling himself handicapped, frustrated, incomplete, projects the idea of what he would wish to be the case as his real self. This would be the projection of the transcendental ego. Strangely enough, in the Kantian tradition, this transcendental ego was viewed as something that the person never could reach; he was more or less condemned to the level of incomplete or inauthentic experience. It was only to the extent that he was able to submit himself to the dictates of the transcendental ego that he became a human being. Kant's very high conception of freedom, as modern philosophy developed, ceased to be attended to and developed, involving as it did this total submission to a fiction.

According to the Nyingmapa tradition of Tibetan Buddhism, when this split occurs, there is just the basic unknowing, *avidya* (*ma-rig-pa* in Tibetan) which is taken as the transcendental self by the empirical self. The empirical self, feeling incomplete or frustrated, mistakes the unknowing for its authentic self. The very clearly thought-out Nyingmapa analysis thus contains an implicit critique of the egoistic philosophy which actually glorifies this unknowing as the ultimate self. According to this analysis, once the positing of the transcendental self occurs, all the further processes of experience involving bodily awareness, etc., are related to this fictitious center.

Q: Can you relate tantra to advaitism?
G: The term *advaita,* as we use it, stems from Shankara's Vedanta. The Buddhists never used this term, but used rather the term *advaya.* Advaya means "not-two"; advaita means "one without a second." The conception of "one without a second" puts us at once into the realm of dualistic fictions. Rather than remaining in immediate experience, with the idea of "one" we posit a definite object. This would then necessarily be over against a definite subject, which is the implication Shankara wanted to deny with the "without a second." By saying "not-two" you remain on solid ground, because "not-two" does not mean "one." That conclusion does not follow.

In the works of Saraha and other Buddhist teachers, it is said that it is impossible to say "one" without prejudgment of experience. But Shankara and his followers were forced by the scriptural authority of the Vedas to posit this One and so were then forced to add the idea "without a second." What they wanted to say was that only Atman is real. Now the logic of their position should force them to then say that everything else is unreal. But Shankara himself is not clear on this point. He re-introduced the idea of illusion which had previously been rejected by him. Now if only Atman is real, then even illusion apart from it is impossible. But he was forced into accepting the idea of illusion. So he was forced into a philosophical position which, if it were to be expressed in a mathematical formula, would make absolute nonsense. So intellectually, in this way, it could be said that the Vedanta is nonsense. But it had tremendous impact; and, as we know, the intellect is not everything. But as the Madhyamika analysis showed, the Vedanta formula simply does not hold water. And Shankara himself, as I said, was not completely clear on this point.

In translating Buddhist texts, it is necessary to take great care with the word "illusion." Sometimes it appears in what is almost an apodictic or judgmental sense. This happens especially in poetry, where one cannot destroy the pattern of the flow of words to make specific philosophical qualifications. But the basic Buddhist position concerning illusion, as prose works are careful to point out, is not the apodictic statement made by the followers of Shankara that the world *is* illusion. The Buddhist position is that the world may be *like* an illusion. There is a huge logical difference between saying the world *is* an illusion and saying the world may be *like* an illusion. The Buddhist position suspends judgment.

So while it has been suggested that Shankara was a crypto-Buddhist, because, in fact, he took over almost the entire epistemological and metaphysical conception of the Buddhists, there remains this very crucial difference.

CHAPTER ELEVEN

Questions and Answers: Rinpoche

Q: What is abhisheka?

R: The literal meaning of *abhisheka* is "anointment." Etymologically it means "sprinkle and pour." It is a sort of emergence into validity, the confirmation of your existence as a valid person as a result of having acknowledged your basic make-up as it is. But abhisheka cannot take place unless the student's training has brought him to a full understanding of the surrendering which is involved in it. He has related his body with the ground by prostrating. He has repeated over and over again the formula: "I take refuge in the Buddha; I take refuge in the Dharma; I take refuge in the Sangha." He has taken refuge in the Buddha as an example; taken refuge in the Dharma as the Path; taken refuge in the Sangha as his companionship on the Path. In that way he has accepted the whole universe as part of his security, warded off the paranoia that comes from the situation of maintaining the ego. In that way he has prepared the space of abhisheka. Having prepared the space, he can relax; he can afford to relax.

Then, the abhisheka takes place as the meeting of two minds. The guru identifies himself with the deity of a particular mandala and encourages the student to do the same. Then the student is crowned and enthroned with all the attributes of that particular symbolism. For instance, the particular deity in question might hold a bell and a vajra in his hands. The guru gives the student a bell and a vajra in order to help him identify himself with the deity. This is the development of what is known in tantric language as vajra pride, indestructible pride. You develop this because you *are* the deity. You have been acknowledged as such by your colleague. He also has accepted you—you are sharing the same space together, so to speak.

Q: Do the various yanas and vehicles intermingle? Are they all part of the Vajrayana?
R: It seems that basically the whole practice is part of the Vajrayana, because you cannot have discontinuity in your practice. You start on the rudimentary level of samsaric ego and use that as the foundation of tantra; then you have the path, then the fruition. But unless you begin with some stuff, something, no matter how apparently crude it is, the process cannot take place. Because you begin with something, that starting point or stepping stone is on the continuity of your path.

Still, however, as I see it, Westerners are largely unprepared for the practices of the Vajrayana at this point, because they have not yet assimilated the basic understanding of Buddhism. In general they do not even have the beginning notions of suffering as explained by the Four Noble Truths. So at this point, the introduction of Buddhism into the West has to be very much on the Hinayana level. People have to relate with the pain of sitting down and meditating and churning out all kinds of material from their minds. This is the truth of suffering, that you are still questioning whether or not the world is the ultimate truth. If the world is the truth, then is pain the truth or is pleasure the truth? People first have to sort out these questions through the use of beginner's practices.

Hopefully, in the next twenty to thirty years Vajrayana principles dealing with the creation of mandalas and identification with deities can be properly introduced. At this point it would be extremely premature. As Professor Guenther said, tantra has been misunderstood from the beginning. So this fundamental misunderstanding has to be corrected first. Having been corrected, then you begin to feel something, then you begin to chew it, swallow it; then you begin to digest it. This whole process will take quite a bit of time.

Q: Can you say something about experiencing deities?
R: Different types of mandalas with different types of deities exist in the iconographical symbolism of tantra. They are associated with all kinds of psychological states. When a person is involved with this symoblism, there is no problem in identifying himself with such deities. There are many different kinds. There is the Father Tantra, the Mother Tantra and the Non-dual Tantra. There is symbolism relating to the five Buddha families: the family of anger, the family of pride, the family of passion, the family of envy and the family of ignorance. When a person has prepared the ground and is able to relax, then he is able to see the highlights of his basic being in terms of these five energies. These energies are not regarded as bad, such that you have to abandon them. Rather, you begin to respect these seeds that you have in yourself. You begin to relate with them as all kinds of deities that are part of your nature. In other words they constitute a psychological picture of you. All this requires a long process.

Q: Could you explain the difference between vajra pride and spiritual pride based on ego? I see numbers of young people involved with spirituality who just seem to be swollen with self-righteousness.
R: Well that seems to be a crucial point. It is the difference, speaking in terms of tantric practice, between the actual faith of identifying with a certain aspect of oneself as a deity and just relating with those deities as one's dream of the future, what one would like to be. Actually, the two situations are very close in some sense because even in the first case one would like to attain enlightenment. Now here the possibility is presented of relating with an enlightened being, or better, of identifying with the enlightened attitude. This brings it home to one that there is such a thing as enlightenment and that, therefore, one can afford to give up one's clingings and graspings. There could quite easily be quite a thin line between this situation and just considering self-righteously that one is already there.

I think ego's version of spiritual pride is based on blind faith, or what is colloquially known as a "love and light trip." This is having blind faith that since one would like to be thus-and-such one already is. In this way one could become Rudra, achieve Rudrahood. On the other hand, vajra pride comes from facing the reality of one's nature. It is not a question of becoming what one would like to be, but rather of bringing one's actual energies to full blossom. The confused ego pride is the indulgence of wishful thinking; it is trying to become something else, rather than being willing to be what one is.

Q: Can you relate the tendency to speed from one thing to the next to the fixity that is central to ego?
R: Fixation could be said to be self-consciousness, which is related with dwelling on something or, in other words, perching on something. That is, you are afraid that you are not secure in your seat, therefore you have to grasp onto something, perch on something. It is something like a bird perching in a tree: the wind might blow the tree, so the bird has to hold on. This perching process, this holding-onto-something process goes on all the time. It is not at all restricted to conscious action, but it goes on inadvertently as well. If the bird falls asleep in the tree, it still perches, still holds on. Like the bird, you develop that extraordinary talent to be able to perch in your sleep. The speed comes in when you are looking constantly for something to perch on, or you feel you have to keep up with something in order to maintain your perch. Speed is the same idea as samsara, going around and around chasing one's own tail. In order to grasp, in order to perch, in order to dwell on something, you need speed to catch up with yourself. So, strangely enough, in regard to ego's game, speed and fixity seem to be complementary.

Q: Is dwelling connected with the lack of perception of impermanence?
R: Yes, that could be said. In Buddhism there is tremendous stress laid on understanding the notion of impermanence. To realize impermanence is to realize that death is taking place constantly and birth is taking place constantly; so there really is nothing fixed. If one begins to realize this and does not push

against the natural course of events, it is no longer necessary to re-create samsara at every moment. Samsara, or the samsaric mentality, is based on solidifying your existence, making yourself permanent, everlasting. In order to do that, since there actually is nothing to grasp onto or sit on, you have to re-create the grasping, the perching, the speeding constantly.

Q: What is the difference between prajna and jnana?
R: Prajna is precision. It is often symbolized as the sword of Manjushri, which severs the root of duality. It is the precision or sharpness of intelligence that cuts off the samsaric flow, severs the aorta of samsara. It is a process of creating chaos in the smooth circulation of maintaining the ego or samsaric mind. This is still a direction, an experience, a learning process, still trying to get at something.

Jnana transcends the learning process, transcends a struggle of any kind; it just is. Jnana is a kind of a self-satisfied samurai—it does not have to fight any more. An analogy used to describe jnana by the Tibetan teacher Petrul Rinpoche is that of an old cow grazing in the meadow quite happily—there is total involvement, total completion. There is no longer any need to sever anything. So jnana is a higher state. It is Buddha-level, whereas prajna is bodhisattva-level.

Q: Does prajna include both intuitional insight and the knowledge that comes out of the rational mind?
R: You see, from the Buddhist point of view, intuition and rationality are something quite different from what is generally understood. Intuition and intellect can only come from the absence of ego. Here it is actually *the* intuition, *the* intellect. They do not relate with the back-and-forth of comparative thinking, which comes from the checking-up process of ego. While you are making the comparative journey, you get confused half-way through so that you lose track of whether you are coming or going. Real intellect skips this entire process. So the ultimate idea of intellect, from the Buddhist point of view, is the absence of ego, which is prajna. But here, in contrast to jnana, there is still a delight in understanding.

Q: Would visualization be on the sambhogakaya level of teaching, since it is based on the experience of shunyata?

R: The practice of visualization is on the dharmakaya level, because until you have reached that level you have not yet worked with the play of phenomena. You have not yet encountered the reality of phenomena as what it is. Up until the shunyata level, you are making a relationship with the phenomenal world; after that, you begin to see the colors, temperatures, textures within the shunyata experience. This is the first glimpse of the possible seed of visualization. Without this foundational development, the practice of visualization could lead to making use of the past and the future, fantasies and memories of shapes and colors. The romantic qualities and desirable aspects of the deities could be focused upon to the extent of losing contact with your basic being. Visualization then becomes a sort of re-creation of the ego.

Q: Is it good practice to meditate while listening to someone speak, you or someone else? Is meditating while listening a contradiction? How should one listen?

R: The traditional literature describes three types of listeners. In one case, one's mind is wandering so much that there's no room at all for anything that's being said. One is just there physically. This type is said to be like a pot turned upside-down. In another case, one's mind is relating somewhat to what's being said, but basically it is still wandering. The analogy is a pot with a hole in the bottom. Whatever you pour in leaks out underneath. In the third case, the listener's mind contains aggression, jealousy, destruction of all kinds. One has mixed feelings about what is being said and cannot really understand it. The pot is not turned upside-down, it doesn't have a hole in the bottom, but it has not been cleaned properly. It has poison in it.

The general recommendation for listening is to try to communicate with the intelligence of the speaker; you relate to the situation as the meeting of two minds. One doesn't particularly have to meditate at that point in the sense that meditation would become an extra occupation. But the speaker can become the meditation technique, taking the place of, let's say, identifying with the breath in sitting meditation. The voice of the speaker would be part of the identifying process, so one should be very close to it as a way of identifying with what the speaker is saying.

Q: Sometimes I have the strange experience in meeting someone, supposedly for the first time, that I've known that person before—a kind of *déjà vu* experience. And even, in some cases, that person will say that it seems to him the same way. It's as though, even though we've never seen each other in this particular life, that we've known each other somewhere before. How do you explain these phenomena?

R: It seems that successive incidents take place and that each incident in the process has a relationship with the past. The process just develops that way. It seems quite simple.

Q: Is it that you bring with you some sort of hangover from the past, some sort of preconception, and it's that that makes you think you've seen that person before?

R: You do that in any case. You bring some energy with you that makes you able to relate to situations as they are. Without that, you wouldn't be here anyway. But there doesn't seem to be anything the matter with that. That energy of being here in the way that we're here is something we have to accept. Partial realization of this might provide you some inspiration. But it doesn't exempt you from having to go through your situation.

Q: It seems very mysterious.

R: If you see the situation completely, somehow that mystery isn't a mystery anymore. It seems mysterious because we don't perceive all the subtleties of things as they are. If you accept the situation it ceases to be a mystery.

Q: You begin to cease in some way to see other people as being completely different people, separate from yourself. At times it seems almost like yourself looking at yourself. Almost, but not quite.

R: At that moment there seems to be a direct contradiction. You see people as separate, but at the same time you see them as part of your innate nature. Somehow the validity of the situation doesn't lie in the logic, but in the perceptions themselves. If there is an actual happening which goes directly against logic, there's nothing wrong with that.

Q: Can you give an example of things going against logic? I've never encountered that.

R: There are all kinds of things like that. You're trying to be an ideal person, trying to bring about ideal karma for yourself, to be good to everybody, etc. Suddenly, you're struck with a tremendous punishment. This kind of thing happens all the time. This is one of the problems unsolved by Christianity. "My people are good Christians, how come they were killed in the war? How does that fit with the divine law of justice?"

Q: I wouldn't say that's a question of logic. Logic doesn't reveal anything about what ought to happen in the world. It has nothing to do with that.

R: Logic comes from expectations. If I fall down I should hurt. We think we should feel pain because if we fall down we *expect* to hurt ourselves. We have set patterns of mind that we've followed all along. We've been conditioned by our culture, our traditions, whatever. This thing is regarded as bad; that thing is regarded as good. If you consider yourself good, then, by this logic, you consider yourself foolproof good. All kinds of good things should happen to you. But there is no fixed doctrine of anything, no kind of exemplary case history of what should be, no manual, no dictionary of what should take place in the universe. Things don't happen according to our conceptualized expectations. That is the very reason why we hasten to make rules for all kinds of things. So if you have an accident, that might be good. It might bespeak something else besides disaster.

Q: You mean that if we have suffering in our lives, that can be a good thing because it provides us with the opportunity to meet the challenge of it and transcend it? That it could stand us in good stead in terms of rebirth?

R: I don't mean to say that things are always for the best. There could be eternally terrifying things. You could be endlessly condemned: since you are suffering in this life, that could cause you to suffer in the next as well. The whole thing is not particularly geared towards goodness. All kinds of things might happen.

Q: When you have partial experiences of non-duality, do you think it's in any way harmful to talk about those experiences? Do you think labeling them can be destructive?

R: I don't think it's particularly destructive or unhealthy, but it might delay the process of development to some extent because it gives you something to keep up with. It makes you try to keep up all the corners and areas of your experiences. It makes you try to keep up with your analysis of the situation; without being poisonous, it is a delaying process. It sort of makes you numb towards relating directly with actual experiences. You don't relate directly because you're wearing a suit of armor. Then you act in accordance with the balance of comfort inherent in the suit of armor. "In accordance with my suit of armor, this experience has to be this way or this way."

Q: How do you take off your armor?
R: It's not exactly a question of taking it off. It is a question of seeing the possibility of nakedness, seeing that you can relate with things nakedly. That way the padding that you wear around your body becomes superfluous at some stage. It's not so much a question of giving up the mask; rather the mask begins to give you up because it has no function for you any more.

Q: Is the urge to explain somehow a function of the ego's wanting to freeze the situation? Establishing where I'm now at rather than just going on and experiencing? What is that? Why is it happening?
R: Essentially because you're relating with some landmark. As long as you're relating to any landmark, any point of reference for comparative study, you're obviously going to be uncomfortable. Because either you're too far from it or you're not too close to it.

Q: A lot of problems in dealing with other people seem to be emotional. Sometimes feelings that are not appropriate to the immediate situation—that are appropriate to something else—just won't disappear. You can know intellectually that they are not appropriate to the situation, but still . . .
R: "Appropriate to the situation" is a questionable idea. To begin with you have to relate to the situation as you see it. You might see that you're surrounded by a hostile environment. The first thing necessary is to study the hostile environement;

see how hostile, how intensive it is. Then you will be able to relate with things.

When you talk about situations, it's quite tricky. We have situations as we would like them to be, as they might be, as they seem to be. It's very up-in-the-air. Situations are not really certain. So before you dance on the ground, you have to check to see if it's safe to dance on, whether it's better to wear shoes or whether you can dance barefoot.

Q: About speaking about one's experiences—if it were in any way harmful to you, would it also be harmful to the person you were talking to? In some circumstances, might it not be a generous thing? It might be useful to them even though it gets you unnecessarily into words. Or would it be harmful to them at the same time?

R: Basically the situation is that there are no separate realities, yours and his, for instance. There's only one reality. If you're able to deal with one end of reality, you're dealing with the whole thing. You don't have to strategize in terms of the two ends. It's one reality. That might make us very uncomfortable, because we would like to be in a position to manipulate and balance various factors so that everything is safe and stable, with things neatly territorialized—his end of the stick, my end of the stick. But basically it's necessary to give up the idea of territory. You are not really dealing with the whole territory anyway, but with one end, not with the peripheries but just with one spot in the middle. But with that one spot in the middle the whole territory *is* covered. So one doesn't have to try to maintain two sides all the time. Just work on the one thing. Reality becomes one reality. There's no such thing as separate realities.

Q: Would you say something about developing mandala in the living situation?

R: That's really what we've been discussing. The complexities of life situations are really not as complicated as we tend to experience them. The complexities and confusions all have their one root somewhere, some unifying factor. Situations couldn't happen without a medium, without space. Situations occur because there's fertile oxygen, so to speak, in the environment to make things happen. This is the unifying factor, the root perspective of the mandala; by virtue of this, chaos is methodically chaotic. For example, we are here and there are many people, a crowd. But each person is coming to some conclusion methodically in relation to the whole thing. That's why we are here. But if an outsider were to pass by and look at the spectacle, it would look like too many people, too complicated. He wouldn't see that there is one situation that we're all interested in, that we're all related to. This is the way it is with everything that happens in life situations. The chaos is methodically chaotic.

Q: You mean it's a matter of different perspectives? Each person has a different reason for being here; if a person looked at it from the outside, he'd see us all sitting here and maybe wouldn't know why. And then . . .
R: I mean we are trying to unify ourselves through confusion.

Q: The more confusion, the more unity?
R: That's what tantric people say.

Q: You mean the more confusion there is, the more difficult it is to stamp a system on reality?
R: You see, chaos has an order by virtue of which it isn't really chaos. But when there's no chaos, no confusion, there's luxury, comfort. Comfort and luxury lead you more into samsara because you are in a position to create more kinds of luxurious possibilities, psychologically, philosophically, physically. You can stretch your legs and invent more gadgets to entertain yourself with. But strangely enough, looking at it scientifically, at the chemistry of it, creating more luxurious situations adds further to your collection of chaos. That is, finally all these luxurious conclusions come back on you and you begin to question them. So you are not happy after all. Which leads you to the further understanding that, after all, this discomfort has order to it.

Q: Is this what you mean when you talk about working with negativity?

R: That's exactly what that is. The tantric tradition talks about transmutation—changing lead into gold.

Q: When you meditate, are you just supposed to space out as much as you can, or ought you to go over your past experiences? It seems more interesting in the direction of spacing out.

R: The basic chemistry of experience, the cosmic law (or whatever you'd like to call it), has its own natural balance to it. You space out, you dream extensively; but the dreaming on and on has no message in it. This is because you failed to relate to the actuality of dreaming, the actuality of spacing out. The point is that you can't reach any sort of infinite point by spacing out, unless you experience the space of earth, which accommodates the actual, solid earthy facts. So the basic chemistry of experience brings you back altogether, brings you down. Buddha's experience is an example of this. Having studied for a long time with mystical teachers, he came to the conclusion that there is no way out. He began to work his own way inward and found there was a way in. Enlightenment is more a way inward than a way out. I don't mean to suggest cultivating a sense of inwardness, but rather relating with the solid, earthy aspect of your experience.

Q: I used to think that there was a way out of conflict. But time went on and it was still there, so I figured there must be a way to live in the midst of conflict. But sometimes it's exhausting trying to keep up with it.

R: But what do you do if there's no conflict?

Q: I can't imagine what it would be like without it. I guess it might not be very alive.

R: It would be deadly. Working with conflict is precisely the idea of walking on the spiritual path. The path is a wild, winding mountain road with all kinds of curves; there are wild animals, attacks by bandits, all kinds of situations cropping up. As far as the occupation of our mind is concerned, the chaos of the path is the fun.

Q: Since Buddhism is starting to be taught here in America,

and it's going to go through interpretations and changes, that being its nature, what pitfalls do you foresee for us in relation to it?

R: There's a danger that people might relate to various expressions about it they encounter rather than to their own experiences of the path. Commentaries and interpretations tend to be colored by sidetracks of all kinds. There is a tremendous danger of people relating to the views around the path rather than the path itself. This is because in the West the teaching is not seen as an understandable thing. It is seen as having some special mystery to it and people are frustrated feeling they're not able to understand it. That frustration looks in all directions trying to find interpretations. When we look somewhere else for a way of interpreting our frustration, when we try to look around it, then the view of the path becomes very much a matter of the roadside scenery rather than the road itself. In the tradition of Buddhism in the past, the path has not been regarded as a sociological or archaeological study of any kind. It has been very much a matter of one's own psychological portrait, one's own psychological geography. If the path is approached in this manner, then one can draw on one's own inspiration, even including the inspiration of one's own cultural background. This does not, however, mean that one should involve oneself with elaborate interpretations relating one's psychology to one's cultural background. This would be another sidetrip. One has to keep to the straight and narrow, keep to the path. Having done that, then one can interpret, because at this point the teaching is no longer a foreign language; it's a very familiar psychological portrait of oneself. The whole process becomes very obvious, very direct, very natural.

Q: Then once you know the strict rules and laws and have the experience, you can start to branch out a little?

R: You can start to branch out in terms of your experiences in daily living, rather than in terms of philosophy or other theoretical constructions. Philosophy or theoretical extrapolations of any kind have no personal relation with you at all. Dealing in terms of these is just collecting further fantasies.

Q: Would you speak about laziness?

R: Laziness is an extremely valuable steppingstone. Laziness is not just lazy, it is extraordinarily intelligent. It can think up all kinds of excuses. It looks for all kinds of ways of manipulating the general situation, the domestic situation, the emotional situation; it invokes your health, your budget; it thinks around all kinds of corners just to justify itself.

At the same time there is a deep sense of self-deception. The application of the logic of laziness is constantly going on in one's own mind. One is constantly having a conversation with oneself, a conversation between one's basic being and one's sense of laziness, setting up the logic which make things seem complete, easy and smooth. But there is a tacit understanding in yourself that, as a matter of fact, this logic is self-deception. This under-the-surface knowledge that it is self-deception, this guilt or discomfort, can be used as a steppingstone to get beyond laziness. If one is willing to do this, what it requires is just acknowledgment of the self-deception. Such acknowledgment very easily becomes a steppingstone.

Q: Do we know what we're doing most of the time?

R: We always know. When we say we don't know what we're doing, it's a big self-deception. We know. As I said earlier, a bird can perch on a tree while he's asleep. We know very well what we are doing, actually.

Q: Awareness is always there, no matter what?

R: There's always ego's awareness, yes. It's always there, a meditative state of its own.

Q: Why is it so hard to face up to that?

R: Because that is our inmost secret, our ultimate treasure. It is that which makes us feel comfortable and vindicated.

Q: Is what we need, then, to take responsibility?

R: Self-deception doesn't relate to the long-term scale on which responsibility is usually seen. It's very limited; it's related to current happenings, actual, small-scale situations. We still maintain our schoolboy qualities, even as grownups.

There is that naughtiness in us always, a kind of shiftiness which is happening all the time, which completely pervades our experience.

Q: In meditation, can it be beneficial to try to relax?
R: From the Buddhist point of view, meditation is not intended to create relaxation or any other pleasurable condition, for that matter. Meditation is meant to be provocative. You sit and let things come up through you—tension, passion or aggression—all kinds of things come up. So Buddhist meditation is not the sort of mental gymnastic involved in getting yourself into a state of relaxation. It is quite a different attitude because there is no particular aim and object, no immediate demand to achieve something. It's more a question of being open.

Shambhala Dragon Editions

The Art of War, by Sun Tzu. Translated by Thomas Cleary.

The Awakened One: A Life of the Buddha, by Sherab Chödzin Kohn.

The Awakening of Zen, by D. T. Suzuki.

Bodhisattva of Compassion: The Mystical Tradition of Kuan Yin, by John Blofeld.

The Buddhist I-Ching. Translated by Thomas Cleary.

The Compass of Zen, by Zen Master Seung Sahn. Foreword by Stephen Mitchell.

Cutting Through Spiritual Materialism, by Chögyam Trungpa.

The Dawn of Tantra, by Herbert V. Guenther and Chögyam Trungpa.

The Diamond Sutra and The Sutra of Hui-neng. Translated by A. F. Price and Wong Mou-lam. Forewords by W. Y. Evans-Wentz and Christmas Humphreys.

The Essence of Buddhism: An Introduction to Its Philosophy and Practice, by Traleg Kyabgon.

The Experience of Insight: A Simple and Direct Guide to Buddhist Meditation, by Joseph Goldstein.

A Flash of Lightning in the Dark of Night: A Guide to the Bodhisattva's Way of Life, by Tenzin Gyatso, the Fourteenth Dalai Lama.

Glimpses of Abhidharma, by Chögyam Trungpa.

Great Eastern Sun: The Wisdom of Shambhala, by Chögyam Trungpa.

The Heart of Awareness: A Translation of the Ashtavakra Gita, translated by Thomas Byrom.

Insight Meditation: The Practice of Freedom, by Joseph Goldstein.

Lieh-tzu: A Taoist Guide to Practical Living, by Eva Wong.

Living with Kundalini: The Autobiography of Gopi Krishna, by Gopi Krishna.

The Lotus-Born: The Life Story of Padmasambhava, by Yeshe Tsogyal. Translated by Erik Pema Kunsang.

Mastering the Art of War, by Zhuge Liang and Liu Ji. Translated and edited by Thomas Cleary.

The Mysticism of Sound and Music, by Hazrat Inayat Khan.

The Myth of Freedom and the Way of Meditation, by Chögyam Trungpa.

Nine-Headed Dragon River: Zen Journals 1969–1982, by Peter Matthiessen.

Returning to Silence: Zen Practice in Daily Life, by Dainin Katagiri. Foreword by Robert Thurman.

Rumi's World: The Life and Work of the Great Sufi Poet, by Annemarie Schimmel.

Shambhala: The Sacred Path of the Warrior, by Chögyam Trungpa.

The Shambhala Dictionary of Buddhism and Zen. Translated by Michael H. Kohn.

The Spiritual Teaching of Ramana Maharshi, by Ramana Maharshi. Foreword by C. G. Jung.

The Sutra of Hui-neng, Grand Master of Zen: With Hui-neng's Commentary on the Diamond Sutra. Translated by Thomas Cleary.

Tao Teh Ching, by Lao Tzu. Translated by John C. H. Wu.

Teachings of the Buddha, revised and expanded edition. Edited by Jack Kornfield.

Vitality, Energy, Spirit: A Taoist Sourcebook. Translated and edited by Thomas Cleary.

The Way of the Bodhisattva: A Translation of the Bodhicharyāvatāra. Translated by the Padmakara Translation Group.

Wen-tzu: Understanding the Mysteries, by Lao-tzu. Translated by Thomas Cleary.

Zen Essence: The Science of Freedom. Translated and edited by Thomas Cleary.